"This book embodies the Jesus way to ...ronment. Written as a partnership betw... a digital native, this book shows how th... the good, critiques the dangers, and sub... ...dden assumptions of this new virtual land. It is therefore essential reading both for those who are disciples of Jesus and for those who want to know what twenty-first-century discipleship can be."

—**David Wilkinson**, St. John's College, Durham University

"Into this place the church is speaking through the real-time, ongoing conversation that is *Following: Embodied Discipleship in a Digital Age*. Jason Byassee and Andria Irwin speak into the space between digital utopians and digital skeptics, modeling biblically grounded, theologically informed wrestling with how the church and Christians live out our mission and vocations amid the current technological revolution. Affirming that Christian faith is an inherently mediated one, Byassee and Irwin provide pathways for us all to draw on some of the best resources of our tradition to live faithfully in the present moment."

—**Deanna A. Thompson**, Lutheran Center for Faith, Values, and Community, St. Olaf College

"*Following* envisions a journey with others toward an uncertain destination. Byassee and Irwin write to cast theological light for our feet in this awkward but exciting expedition of faith in our digital culture. As fellow pilgrims on the way, they invite us into an urgent conversation that is sober yet hopeful and that may land us at an Emmaus table or an online platform with surprise vistas of Christ."

—**Andrew Byers**, Ridley Hall, Cambridge; author of *TheoMedia: The Media of God in the Digital Age*

FOLLOWING

PASTORING FOR LIFE

Theological Wisdom for Ministering Well
Jason Byassee, Series Editor

Aging: Growing Old in Church
by Will Willimon

Birth: The Mystery of Being Born
by James C. Howell

Disability: Living into the Diversity of Christ's Body
by Brian Brock

Friendship: The Heart of Being Human
by Victor Lee Austin

*Recovering: From Brokenness and Addiction
to Blessedness and Community*
by Aaron White

FOLLOWING

EMBODIED
DISCIPLESHIP IN
A DIGITAL AGE

JASON BYASSEE AND ANDRIA IRWIN

Baker Academic
a division of Baker Publishing Group
Grand Rapids, Michigan

© 2021 by Jason Byassee and Andria Irwin

Published by Baker Academic
a division of Baker Publishing Group
PO Box 6287, Grand Rapids, MI 49516-6287
www.bakeracademic.com

Printed in the United States of America

Library of Congress Cataloging-in-Publication Data
Names: Byassee, Jason, author. | Irwin, Andria, author.
Title: Following : embodied discipleship in a digital age / Jason Byassee and Andria Irwin.
Description: Grand Rapids, Michigan : Baker Academic, a division of Baker Publishing Group, [2021] | Series: Pastoring for life | Includes bibliographical references and index.
Identifiers: LCCN 2020053200 | ISBN 9781540962270 (paperback) | ISBN 9781540964236 (casebound)
Subjects: LCSH: Discipling (Christianity) | Technology—Religious aspects—Christianity. | Social media—Religious aspects—Christianity. | Pastoral theology.
Classification: LCC BV4520 .B93 2021 | DDC 248.4—dc23
LC record available at https://lccn.loc.gov/2020053200

21   22   23   24   25   26   27   7   6   5   4   3   2   1

For Leighton Ford, who mastered high-tech evangelism
and then gave it up for face-to-face friendship

And for Fleming Rutledge, surprising
and surprised social media preacher
—JB

For Allison, Marc, and Jennifer,
whose collective counsel helped free my voice
—AI

Contents

Series Preface

One of the great privileges of being a pastor is that people seek out your presence in some of life's most jarring transitions. They want to give thanks. Or cry out for help. They seek wisdom and think you may know where to find some. Above all, they long for God, even if they wouldn't know to put it that way. I remember phone calls that came in a rush of excitement, terror, and hope. "We had our baby!" "It looks like she is going to die." "I think I'm going to retire." "He's turning sixteen!" "We got our diagnosis." Sometimes the caller didn't know why they were calling their pastor. They just knew it was a good thing to do. They were right. I will always treasure the privilege of being in the room for some of life's most intense moments.

And, of course, we don't pastor only during intense times. No one can live at that decibel level all the time. We pastor in the ordinary, the mundane, the beautiful (or depressing!) day-by-day most of the time. Yet it is striking how often during those everyday moments our talk turns to the transitions of birth, death, illness, and the beginning and end of vocation. Pastors sometimes joke, or lament, that we are only ever called when people want to be "hatched, matched, or dispatched"—born or baptized, married, or eulogized. But those are moments we share with all humanity, and they are good moments in which to do gospel work. As an American, it feels perfectly natural to ask a couple how they met. But a South African friend told me he feels this is exceedingly intrusive! What I am really asking is how someone met God as they met the person to whom they have made lifelong promises. I am asking about transition and encounter—the tender places where the God of cross and resurrection meets us. And I am thinking about how to bear witness amid the transitions that are our lives. Pastors are the ones who get phone calls at these moments and have the joy, burden, or just plain old workaday job of showing up with oil for anointing, with prayers, to be a sign of the Holy Spirit's overshadowing goodness in all of our lives.

I am so proud of this series of books. The authors are remarkable, the scholarship first-rate, the prose readable—even elegant—the claims made ambitious and then well defended. I am especially pleased because so often in the church we play small ball. We argue with one another over intramural matters while the world around us struggles, burns, ignores, or otherwise proceeds on its way. The problem is that the gospel of Jesus Christ isn't just for the renewal of the church. It's for the renewal of the cosmos—everything God bothered to create in the first place. God's gifts are not *for* God's people. They are *through* God's people, *for* everybody else. These authors write with wisdom, precision, insight, grace, and good humor. I so love the books that have resulted. May God use them to bring glory to God's name, grace to God's children, renewal to the church, and blessings to the world that God so loves and is dying to save.

Jason Byassee

Acknowledgments

I (Jason) am grateful first to Andria Irwin for being willing to write this book with me. As I sent her internet link after internet link I realized what I had become—the weird elder relative who thinks everything on the web is interesting and passes it right along. Thanks for letting me be your weird uncle. I love that moment when I was on my phone in Epiphany Chapel *during worship* and you turned to me and said, "You know you're terrible with that thing, right?"

I had the benefit of being the youngest staff member at several media outlets early in the digital era and so being forced to figure out blogging. The *Christian Century* nudged me to start what was then called *Theolog* and what came to be the *Christian Century* network of blogs. It has some really good writers now. For a time, it just had me and whomever I could manipulate into writing for me for no pay. Wondering what we were doing online got me asking questions about what digital technology is for. I am grateful for those opportunities (and I owe some friends some money!). Thanks to my longtime colleague and friend there Amy Frykholm for her help editing this volume.

My next calling was to Leadership Education at Duke Divinity School where I edited (you guessed it) a blog for faithandleadership .com. Here I started to write about life online versus life in-person for the *Christian Century*, for *Faith & Leadership*, and for other outlets, like *Christian Reflections* at Baylor University and *First Things*. I tried out the ideas that appear in this book with audiences at Duke; at

St. Olaf's conference on worship, liturgy, and the arts; and at Western Theological Seminary, and I am grateful for the hospitality in each place and the patience of my listeners. Then I became pastor at Boone United Methodist and nudged the congregation to do more ministry online, though nothing compared to what we're all doing post-COVID-19. I am grateful for the chance to speak about my ideas for Andy Langford's Connexion13 gathering at Central United Methodist in Concord, North Carolina, and for Andy Crouch's invitation to Laity Lodge in Kerrville, Texas, to discuss technology with the great Eugene Peterson and with Albert Borgmann, the Yoda of this conversation. Audiences at Bay View Chautauqua in Michigan and the Western Pennsylvania Conference of the United Methodist Church were also patient in hearing me out and correcting me often. Thank you all.

My profound thanks go to Verity Jones, who won a Lilly grant to explore technology and the church with the New Media Project, housed for a time at Union Theological Seminary in New York City and then at Christian Theological Seminary in Indianapolis. Every idea I ever had about technology was tested out, challenged, and refined by my fellow Fellows: Kathryn Reklis, Monica Coleman, Lerone Martin, and Jim Rice. Thank you, Verity and friends.

As with everything I do, I am grateful to Jaylynn Byassee and to our sons, Jack, Sam, and Will. Thank you to Richard Topping for his remarkable leadership of the Vancouver School of Theology, gathering a community where I could teach students like Andria and learn with them on projects like this. Thank you to Dave Nelson and Baker Academic for the opportunity to edit the Pastoring for Life series and to include this volume in its midst. Thank you to the many interview subjects and friends quoted in these pages.

And thank you to my dedicatees—Leighton Ford and Fleming Rutledge. Friendship may be God's greatest gift to us.

———

I (Andria) would like to acknowledge that this book would not have been possible without Dave Nelson and Baker Academic's faith in me as a first-time author and the support of my coauthor Jason Byassee. When Jason dropped into my DMs (direct messages) from the back

pew of a sanctuary asking, "Are we really still talking about this?" I
did not ever expect him to take my "we need to say even more" quip
seriously. He did, and he has continued to take me seriously in all
my iterations throughout this process, particularly when I disagreed
with him. I am grateful for his mentorship, wisdom, and friendship.
Even the links to news articles.

My work on technology and the church would not have been possible without the congregational encouragement of Highlands United
Church and their lead minister, Will Sparks. Thank you for allowing
me to break important things and for later helping me fix them. To
Rob Crosby-Shearer and Treena Duncan, thank you for supporting
authentic online ministry long before we were forced to. To Kerry
Karram and the wider HUC congregation, thank you for trusting me
with your worship experience and your stories. You are the reason
that the content of these pages matters. Debra Bowman, thank you
for your mentorship, your edits, and your honesty.

To the professors at the Vancouver School of Theology (including Jason) who guided me and who inspired me to ask bigger and
bolder questions of God with digital ministry as my focus, thank you
for your curiosity and your office hours. Your teaching, invitations,
encouragements, and feedback helped shape the content of these
chapters. Sorry for double-dipping.

For those who agreed to take yet another Zoom meeting and answer endless questions about themselves and their online practices
in interviews, I am deeply appreciative. Your personal and pastoral
ministries are a blessing to the communities surrounding you, and
I eagerly await the next time we can speak. For the friends and colleagues on whom I informally imposed these conversations, thank
you for your vulnerability and enthusiasm. To the Christian Ladies
Wine Club (AG, AF, LR, FK), this book was written by your prayers.

Most of all, thank you to my family for agreeing to come second
for a little while. Sandi (mum) and Nick (dad), you let me stay in the
guest room so I could get feedback at midnight on my latest chapter,
and you always said it was "great enough!" so I could get some sleep.
Steve—a lifetime of thank-yous for walking this road with me.

Finally, to the prophets and the pioneers: some seed fell on good
soil.

Introduction

The End Is Near

It was a really long meeting. The kind that the COVID-19 pandemic may have exiled to Zoom forever. Andria and I both had to sit and listen to a script being read about the dangers of social media. The room full of ministers our parents' and grandparents' ages nodded their heads and asked ancient questions. They hardly knew what Twitter was, and yet they were being encouraged to fear it all the more: The internet is forever. Don't embarrass yourself. Don't embarrass your church. Don't misrepresent the faith. Don't break professional boundaries and get too close to parishioners personally. Don't, don't, don't.

Chatting via Twitter DM—the very sort of social media distraction I discourage in the classroom—Andria's and my bitmojis rolled our eyes. This was the wrong way to talk about technology. It really isn't that big a deal. It's great in fact. Now we can pass notes in class without even moving! We can access all of Christian tradition and every church's sermons today with a touch of a screen. We can worship despite a global pandemic. The refrain shouldn't be "Don't, don't, don't"; it should be . . . well, *what*? How do we talk about technology hopefully? We nearly had a book proposal sketched out in the DMs about how the church can use technology, with hope, rather than being used by it. This is that book.

I sometimes joke that I (Jason) have been pondering a book on God and technology since before Andria was born. It's not quite true. I'm a digital immigrant, with full memory of rotary phones and life before email. Andria is a digital native who has lived nearly her entire life online. I didn't start pondering this book at fifteen. But something did happen around that time, as Bill Gates's dream of a computer in every household arrived and the nascent internet started crowding out physical encyclopedias. It became mandatory to pursue digital technology. Not to do so was not just to be a Luddite. It was to do harm to your children, to slow down their "progress," to cut oneself off from the world and its economic opportunities.

To refuse technology now is to be genuinely sectarian. You can do it, but people will regard you the way many (unfairly) do the Amish or Haredi Jews: countercultural, momentarily intriguing, and ultimately irrelevant. We are not free to be without the devices that rule our lives with screens. We must plug in.

This is partly due to what Christians should see is a false eschatology. Technology has always announced itself with fanfare as though Jesus's kingdom has arrived, salvation is here, and all is well. Hence the incomprehension, even indignation, when anyone tries to absent themselves from it. This habit of speaking of a technological advance as though it were the returned Messiah is not new. Witness this 1850 quotation from a Methodist missionary reflecting on the invention of the telegraph:

> This noble invention is to be the means of extending civilization, republicanism, and Christianity over the earth. It must and will be extended to nations half-civilized, and thence to those now savage and barbarous. Our government will be the grand center of this mighty influence. . . . The beneficial and harmonious operation of our institutions will be seen, and similar ones adopted. Christianity must speedily follow them, and we shall behold the grand spectacle of a whole world, civilized, republican, and Christian. . . . Wars will cease from the earth. Men "shall beat their swords into plough shares, and their spears into pruning-hooks." . . . Then shall come to pass the millennium.[1]

Of course, not all responded to the telegraph with such eschatological hyperventilation. Henry David Thoreau, upon being told that the device would allow Maine and Texas to communicate with one another instantly, asked the appropriate question: What if Maine and Texas have nothing to say to one another?[2] Some have responded to technological advance with apocalyptic terminology that suggests not jubilation but anxiety. U. S. Grant, upon seeing a train for the first time in his life in 1839, marveled, "It annihilates space."[3] The known world was now different. Wendell Berry, regarding a tech marvel a century later—the interstate highway system—observed that it made near things far away and far things near.[4] Communities too poor to resist the build were often divided, atomized, and left more violent. And such communities were disproportionately Black (see here Chicago's West Side). But suburbs and city centers were made closer for commuters' convenience.

Technology always claims to bring eschatological significance: greater prosperity, ease, and happiness. Few would go back on medical advances, fewer still among those not fortunate enough to be effortlessly healthy. Communications advances, from the telegraph to the telephone to television to the internet, are more complicated. We will deal with those the most in this book. We can access all the world's treasures on our devices, and yet we are bored still. Transportation advances are even more complex. Advances in navigation and shipbuilding were a marvel. The same ships that first traversed the globe also brought diseases and territorial acquisition to the Americas and chattel slavery to Africa. Technology often just makes more of us. And we human beings are sinners—especially when we think we are not. Technology promises to distribute largesse and to fend off disease, discomfort, ignorance, and boredom. But it hides outrages. Do you know which minerals must be mined for that little supercomputer in your pocket, who owns the land those mines are on, and who does the labor?

I sure don't. Ooh, a ping! Someone just posted something interesting on Twitter . . .

The internet's designers and its wealthiest investors hail their work in religious categories. What other category could they use? The internet claims to be everywhere, knowing all things, not quite omnipotent, but not far off. Confident futurists imagine a day when our memories can be uploaded and our individual consciousnesses preserved after death. Democracy advocates hope that the web will keep pressure on despots, alleviate harassment of activists, and make the world a more open place. It will democratize access to education as billions more can tap into Harvard from their smartphones. Perhaps such advocates have been unaware that totalitarians can use the web just as effectively or more so to surveil those same activists, spread disinformation, and infect democracy with mistrust. Thoreau was sanguine about eschatological claims for his day's various gizmos—lamenting "improved means to unimproved ends."[5] He was wrong about Maine and Texas though. They wanted to sell each other stuff. But he was right about technology's inability to say *what* we should want to want or why.

The web can give you all the information in the world, but it can't make you wise.

And this is precisely our greatest worry with technology: its omnivorous pretension. Technology claims to be able to fix all that ails us. Those who exempt themselves from it are backward barbarians. Those who lead the way in this industry are deserved billionaires—we should hang on their every word (hmm—who exactly designed the systems by which we listen to them?).

In the Bible, Jesus promises several times to give believers whatever they want (e.g., Matt. 7:7; 18:19; Luke 11:9). This is confusing. Anyone who has prayed has had the experience of not receiving an answer or at least not the answer they want. Jesus also commands us to take up our cross and follow him, to love our enemies, to be part of a kingdom with the rich thrown down and the poor exalted. One preacher squared the circle this way: God gives us what we want, *after God changes our wants around.*[6] Christianity is about reorienting and healing our desire. Rather than desiring wealth and the cruel death of our enemies, we come to desire what God longs for: creation healed, our enemies blessed, life with the poor, love of God and neighbor.

Pray for that, and God will grant it. Eventually.

The web also claims to give us whatever we want whenever we want it. If we have the cash. From the way we all go about staring at our screens, a visitor from Mars might think we worship these little gods in our pockets that glow in our hands and draw our eyes. Critics of the web point out that the world's best engineers have designed these systems to addict us. Those push notifications, those "likes" on social media, all of it gives us a dopamine hit. Trying to turn away is like an addict turning down the pipe. It's really, really hard. The devices make us, in Sherry Turkle's matchless phrase, live "alone together."[7] We pay attention to some contextless module of information instead of the flesh-and-blood human being in front of us. We get jittery if we haven't checked email in ten or twenty seconds. In her recent acknowledgments Zadie Smith, the great British writer, thanked an app that disabled her internet for allowing her to get her book done.[8] That's about our best hope: using technology to subvert technology's hold on us.

One Twitter handle will tweet you a daily reminder that you are going to die. Not a bad start. And this is the trick with technology— to use it to remind us of our creatureliness.

Christianity is the sort of faith best understood by saying what it's *not* than what it *is*. Heresies come from *somewhere*—some strand in Scripture or tradition or some practice yanked out of context and magnified out of proportion. Heresies are usually simplifying movements—one part of Christian tradition yanked out and made the whole in an effort to simplify matters, when that one part should instead be kept as part of the paradoxical mess of an irreducibly complex entirety.[9] Is God one or three? Heretics choose one at the expense of the other; the Orthodox, confusingly, insist on both. Is Christ human or divine? Ditto. Holding fast to one piece of Christian tradition and eschewing the rest, we've learned, is to tear the thing apart.

One particular heresy that keeps coming back around is called Gnosticism—a heresy that says salvation is a rescue from the space-time world of bodies, creation, and bread and wine and water. Watch *The Matrix* or *The Truman Show* and you've got Gnosticism: the world we experience is a lie; we must escape to the real one. Our digital age threatens to be a new Gnostic heresy—a false claim of salvation that the church should resist. Even Hollywood knows Gnosticism has Christianesque appeal: Who is Neo's love interest in *The Matrix*? Trinity. Who is the keeper of Truman's world? Christof.

Gnostics can find Scripture to support their escapism easily enough. In John's Gospel, Jesus fulminates against "the world"; the Gospels contain suggestions that extra *secret* knowledge might have been imparted to only a few of the disciples (e.g., John 21:25: "There are also many other things that Jesus did"). The way Christians often speak of heaven as a sort of escape route for individual souls sounds not a little gnostic too. The church has stood at this precipice before, and it has fallen right in.

Sometimes despite ourselves, we remember that Christian redemption has always been full-blooded, a new creation, a coming heaven and earth. Our Gnostic tendencies are undone by our connection to our Jewish forebears. Judaism is good ballast against floating off into the ether. The internet cuts the chain entirely. Thinkers of this kind insist they will never teach "embodied" or "sacramental" theology online.[10] For all the wonders of the internet, it is not a place where you can eat a meal or baptize someone—not yet anyway. Online church communities seek ways around it. One community says they mail elements to parishioners or fly to baptize them or ask folks to go to the cupboard and come back to eat together. But however much of our lives are possible online, our bodies have a stubborn . . . bodiliness about them. At one gathering of academics, John Milbank, the leading Radical Orthodox light in the UK, and Cornel West, the philosopher-activist from the US, "met" in the Q&A. West asked Milbank an intriguing question: What are you so afraid of? (Not a bad question to take the temperature of any human being or community.) Milbank responded: a world where people want online sex more than the embodied kind.[11] That is, a Gnostic world of purported escape from bodies, creation, food and drink, and love.

If Christian theologians have sounded apocalyptic in their rejection of technology at times, nonreligious scholars can sound even worse—they have to *borrow* Christian terminology to have a big enough stick to beat the devil with. Witness Sven Birkerts thundering away like any apocalyptic preacher, despite seeming to have no actual religious commitments of his own:

> The devil no longer moves about on cloven hooves, reeking of brimstone. He is an affable, efficient fellow. He claims to help us all along

to a brighter, easier future, and his sales pitch is very smooth. . . .
Fingers tap keys, oceans of fact and sensation get downloaded, are
dissolved through the nervous system. Bottomless wells of data are
accessed and manipulated, everything flowing at circuit speed. Gone
the rock in the field, the broken hoe, the grueling distances. . . . From
deep in the heart I hear the voice that says, "Refuse it."[12]

This is not unlike the language of the Hebrew prophets or John the
Baptist or the desert monks and nuns who imitated them by flee-
ing from the world and giving birth to monasticism. We need that.
One refrain in this book will be that we need some people to refuse
technology as entirely as they can, just as we need some Christians
to forswear money, sex, and power for a deeper embrace with Jesus.
Protestantism is a five-hundred-year experiment to see whether we
can have Christianity without anybody becoming monks or nuns.
The early returns aren't good. Birkerts has no monastics, and so he
has to demand a thing for which he sees little evidence—a hopeless
apocalypticism, that.

   We see in these various rhetorical rejections of technology a revival
of the ancient Christian heresy of Manicheism. This was a view (ap-
pealing to many in the ancient Mediterranean) that the world is made
up of some things that are essentially good (us!) and others that are
essentially bad (our enemies!). An elaborate cosmology followed in its
own time and place, but for followers the result was that believers had
to flee from this world and all its materiality. Creation was a sort of
cosmic accident. Any continuity of it furthers a mistake. Procreation is
bad—it entraps more souls in bodies. So too such bodily lamentables
as eating and drinking—the sorts of things Jesus spent his time on
(there is a reason he is accused of being a drunkard and a glutton!).
Cosmologically, light is trapped in darkness and needs to get free but
cannot. In more colloquial terms, Manicheism makes the mistake of
thinking of some things as essentially good and others as essentially
evil. There is no essential evil in Christian thought. All of creation is
good but fallen and is being redeemed by Christ. You can't go pick
up a handful of evil. Everything that is, by virtue of its existence, is
good. It also tends toward decay. The world is good, beautiful even, but
mortal. We might even say it is wounded but being healed by Christ.

Too categorical a denunciation of technology risks Manicheism. It overlooks the goods born into our lives by technology—goods like medicine and transport and communication and alleviated toil. Who would give up an aged photo of a long-lost beloved? It almost participates in the person's memory. Categorical denunciations risk hypocrisy when these screeds are published in books, written on computers, tweeted about. They ignore the fact that human beings are tool-making animals. Israel's Scripture speaks with beauty of the skill of those who beautify the temple with their technology in Exodus, of those who mine the treasures of the earth in Job, of those who play music to the Lord in the Psalms. The first maker of things may be the Lord himself, sewing together animal skins to replace Adam and Eve's pitiful fig leaves when they are expelled from the garden. Intellectuals have always feared technology. Plato worried about writing since it would cause folks' memories to decay. He was absolutely right, of course. The medieval Catholic Church feared the printing press would corrode their authority, again, full props for prophetic insight. Martin Marty points out that every technological revolution in American history has brought a new outbreak of fundamentalism.[13] People who were formerly isolated can find one another, and are horrified, or they can collaborate. The progress narrative of American optimism assumes this makes the world better—kill bad speech with more free speech. The internet itself may be undoing this optimism—more "free speech" just leads to hate radio, cable news, internet trolling, and Russian bots. Critics of technology are usually more right than wrong, but they forget the simple reality that people embrace the alphabet, the printed book, and the radio because they make our lives better. The church longs to communicate the gospel—how can we not use these gifts?

Categorical denunciation of digital technology misunderstands the very nature of the church. Christianity has always been a virtual body. Saint Paul wrote letters to Christians he would never meet in the flesh assuming a sort of authority in a community that includes them. The church is universal in time and space, using the best technology then available (letters, carried over Roman roads and on ships over the Mediterranean) to tie congregations together. The Bible often laments that virtual communication is inferior to embodied presence.

Yet these consolation prizes, second-best letters, are canonized and called *Scripture*—the very word of God. Many of our greatest texts from the patristic era started as letters from one bishop to another congregation—perhaps one he would never meet in person but to whom he would be united in mutual prayer.[14] Christianity is an epistolary faith, based on writings to and from friends who know one another in the flesh and others who do not—yet are not for that reason any less part of the body of Christ.

Throughout this book we will catalogue ways that the church's ministry becomes possible in cyberspace that would have been impossible beforehand. We have to be alert to new corruptions in that newly possible space, of course. Yet to forswear it entirely is unwise. To wit: some of the best websites on the planet are run by monks and nuns. These fleers of imperial money, sex, and power know their form of life appeals still. They want people to know about it, so they use the web. We can hardly accuse them of disembodied, Gnostic escapism—at least not any more than we can accuse the church fathers and mothers of that.

The goal of this book is a middle way between the heresies of Gnosticism and Manicheism. A practical, hope-filled approach to our online tools that keeps them squarely in their place—as tools—rather than as our masters. Tools that come from and serve the fleshly body of Christ on its way to redeeming the world.

Note the objection here is not to the harm technology can do. We need people who say "no" altogether. They will devote their lives entirely to prayer, service, and holiness. All of us need to do that at times, for a time. Just as everyone must pray and fast and abstain from sex for a time, all of us must abstain from technology at times. In prayer, for example. Yes, the Bible can be accessed online, but so too can all our digital communication—it's just too tempting to break communion with God to commune with Insta. Teenagers often go without sleep so they can text in the middle of the night. Over meals. In class. There are places that call for our undivided attention. These devices dilute it, divide it, inviting commercial advertisements and diversion into every formerly sacred space. Refuse that, please. Nicholas Carr has helpfully written of the way web grazing has cost him the ability to concentrate on demanding texts for hours at a time.[15]

Birkerts worries that the loss of the ability to be bored deprives us of the sort of deep attention necessary for genuine creativity. They are both right. We must turn off the devices to read Tolstoy or to create the next Tolstoy.

And then we have to use them to do the things Jesus commanded: to love God and neighbor. To go into all the world baptizing. To witness to the repair of creation through a resurrected rabbi. To be Jesus's own body in the world, working alongside as the Holy Spirit knits back together everything we've ruined. That's the right eschatology—over against Gnostic escape (the internet is saving us!) or Manichean rejection (the internet is damning us!). Jesus is saving us. Now, having taken a deep breath, how can we use these devices in his agenda of redeeming the world?

This book will explore the goods that digital technology makes possible in our lives, and it will also attend to technology's profound dangers. We will do so in conversation, occasionally breaking with the predominant voice in a chapter to disagree in a separate section. In chapter 1 Andria will argue that Christian discipleship is always a matter of putting on a new and unfamiliar self. In chapter 2 she will show how some pastors have navigated having a pastoral persona and also a social media one. In chapter 3 I (Jason) will offer some categories for how to think about church and technology—and how not to. In chapter 4 I will suggest some ways for how to think through online technology's effect on our families. In chapter 5 Andria will think through friendship in light of technology. In chapter 6 Andria, as a full-fledged internet pastor, will attend to the Great Commission and mission in this new day. In chapter 7 I will issue a halting "no" to the question of whether we can commune online, and in a separate section Andria will respond with a "but of course." In chapter 8 I will address preaching online, and in our conclusion we will circle back around to God (who, we hope, we have never left in the first place), for the God of the gospel never appears unmediated. Throughout, we seek to ask how these potentially disembodied media can be turned for good use in an embodied, incarnational faith.

As a digital immigrant and a digital native, respectively, we will write in our own voices, with space for the other to interject on particular points of disagreement. We will draw on learned essays, interviews we've conducted with faithful practitioners, and our own intuition (challenged by one another and the churches we've served). Forgive us if we repeat ourselves occasionally. Karl Barth said we can only repeat ourselves (and then showed what he meant with ten thousand pages of *Church Dogmatics*!). We hope our way of writing will imitate and then inspire the sort of dialogue necessary in the church to discern how to receive the jarring gift of technology. We will close each chapter with a question or two meant to ignite small group conversation. For example . . .

- How might we use technology, perhaps despite its intentions, to trick ourselves into a more embodied life of discipleship?

ONE

Putting on the New Self

The opening chapter of Genesis seems like as good a place as any to begin a book on discipleship in a digital age. You will notice that I (Andria) will sway slightly from Jason's more critical approach in the chapters to follow through one constant refrain: this place, and who we are in it, has been proclaimed good (Gen. 1:31). The digital age, as we are calling it, has extended an invitation to bring our whole selves, made and blessed in the divine image, into a new place where we can choose who exactly we want to be. Who we are in such a technological time isn't just a question for new generations, digital literacy classes, and social media marketers. It's a question for all of us, especially those of us who are Christians, as we work to discern how to tell our story in a loud and hyper-distracted world.

There is a wild permission available in this place for those who care to take it—a permission not only to follow but to teach, to serve, and to love. How we do this is changing every day, but the story we tell stays the same. Before we tell that story, however, we should know ourselves, and that journey of a life is different here in the digital landscape than anywhere else.

In September 1999, a young valley girl opened up a Hotmail account with the username "californiasurfangel18." Sandy brown hair, fingernails bitten to the quick, and shoulders twice as wide as she was tall, she chose to imagine herself instead like a character in a Sweet Valley High novel: tan, athletic, popular, and perhaps named Jessica.

Three years earlier, in a warehouse in Santa Clara County, Sabeer Bhatia and Jack Smith had successfully launched Hotmail.com, a first of its kind—anonymous, easily accessible, entirely remote, and free email service that would change the way people communicated overnight. Now, as Jessica launched herself into a new life on the World Wide Web, Bhatia and Smith celebrated the launch of their newest service, an instant messaging program they called MSN Messenger.

Californiasurfangel18 sat in front of her computer monitor on a Friday afternoon, painstakingly constructing her first ever MSN Messenger name. It had to be something clever. The popular ASL (Age, Sex, Location) wouldn't do. It had to reflect the "real" her; the person she aspired to be, not the freckle-faced girl with chapped lips and barrettes in her hair. Like many of her friends, Jessica began her journey of self-exploration on this virtual platform. It would not be the last time she put on a new self (Col. 3:10).

It worked. For a whole weekend Jessica was the new girl in school. She befriended the cheerleaders, the ballerinas, the entire roster of the boys' junior hockey team—and they all talked to her. For three days, Jessica was able to virtually embody her wildest dreams. The chance to shed the skin she had been given and to step into a masked version of herself left her feeling, perhaps for the first time, worthy.

Can you remember the last time you felt as worthy as God declared you? Good without adornment or status, simply deserving of love by virtue of existing? It is not likely, in our consume-and-compare culture, that we experience the assurance of the opening chapter of Genesis with any form of regularity—at least not when we spend our time immersed in the highlight reels of others. We cry out *not enough!* in the face of what we perceive others to have. Or, at the very least, we clamber over piles of dirty laundry with our laptops for a conference call to settle in the one corner of the house that might, to the untrained eye, appear "tidy." *Not enough!* A challenge is set before us in this digital age. The children of postmodernity in our midst (Gen Y, Gen Z, Gen Alpha) have the particular task of becoming in a world focused on belonging.

Such a world is not as it might seem. Belonging in our Western culture is not the biblical concept of being neither slave nor free, gentile nor Jew. Instead, it is the concept that launched a thousand acronyms—ASAP, MIA, FOMO, YOLO, BRB—abbreviations of our most valued sentiments, which would seem to be production and prominence based.

We are made to feel, through no fault of our own, that we are not enough simply by way of seeing what we think others are. We bury our faces into our hands, pose ourselves in lament, and pray to be better, bolder, more productive next week, yet we arise on Monday the same as we were before. In Jessica's case, that was a young girl living in a valley not like the one that would become known as Silicon Valley but instead one that runs along the North Thompson River in the westernmost province of Canada, twelve hundred miles away from the warm surf of the California Pacific. Not named Jessica at all but Andria (me again!).

To belong, some of us are willing to do anything except become the selves already pronounced beloved by our maker. Our identities are designed through the slow, lifelong penning of stories, creating caricatures of ourselves that feel worthy of the lives we think we should be living. We wear, according to modern psychology, masks of ourselves. A kind of costume parade that lasts, hellishly, from birth until death.

This idea of trying on the self is not new. In the sixteenth century Italians popularized the masquerade, a celebration during which masking one's identity could encourage people to live and let live. By shielding our faces, the beasts of ourselves could run wild into the night, while our dignity could awake the next morning intact, the faint howl of a headache ringing in the distance.

The freedom of this kind of anonymity was a siren call into the online world in the late '90s and early 2000s. Forums, blogging, and multiuser experiences became places where people could be themselves or not, with no one the wiser. This falsely utopic world was brimming with possibilities for manipulation, abuse of power, and crime, but it also created an environment that allowed people, some for the first time, to start over. For those with genuine intentions of alternative expression and re-creation, this fantastical place of faceless personalities was one of welcome and escape. People were welcomed into this community and *seen* in ways they had never been seen before. At the same time, this new realm offered respite from an unwanted body or persona or circumstance. It was the heaven we grew up hearing about—the one where our physical and emotional ailments would ail us no longer and we would be free from the conditions that traumatize us here on earth.

This kind of co-reality in which people were able to exist in two places at once, as two people at once, was a new game. People endeavored to play creator of themselves and their lives in ways that took little effort and had the potential of immediate gratification. You, too, could have the beautiful girl if you showed her a photo of a man twenty years your junior and told her about your offshore accounts (catfish). You, too, could finally have your controversial opinion heard in the comment section of the local newspaper despite them never putting your op-eds to print (troll). You, too, could offer self-help coaching to unsuspecting, hurting individuals despite never having had any coaching yourself (scam). Dividing the self into split experiences of reality is something we have seen go violently wrong. Instead of working through selfish or harmful desires in the safety of professional or peer accompaniment, the physical self represses these yearnings while the online self acts out. It is easy to find horror stories of fantasies running rampant on the darknet and of abusers lurking behind innocent online avatars, and we wonder what the justification for anonymity ever was.

Yearning to be a new person, however, is not inherently dangerous or deceptive. It is our core identity as disciples of Jesus to be like him (John 15:12) and to grow in our desires and actions until we find ourselves unable to be separated from our true identity as children of God. Until we know how to make this transition, however, we will not use the tools we have for their highest potential.

Into this place the church can speak. Created in Jesus for good works (Eph. 2:10), we follow the One who tells us the troubles of the world are cast aside through him (John 16:33). While the internet certainly has its dark corners, so does our human experience. The formative work of Christian community is to accompany us through the discerning moments, turning us always toward our greater identity—

an identity that openly celebrates the Divine's image of life for us—one in which we feel that we are enough.

Peter Rollins, the provocative Irish storyteller and lecturer who has penned seasonal devotionals with titles like "Atheism for Lent,"[1] recounts a supposedly true story of a twentieth-century theologian who was discreetly invited to participate in a masked orgy involving everyone who was anyone at the time. The theologian, disregarding the rules of the soirée, showed up wearing nothing—not even something to conceal his identity. When the shocked host pulled him aside to tell him the event was a masked one (because arriving nude was the normal part here), the theologian allegedly responded, "Why, my dear friend, what you see *is* my mask."[2]

The shift from anonymity to exposure came almost overnight in 2004 with the introduction of Mark Zuckerberg's Facebook. The emergence of this new social media, along with its user agreements and browser tracking, named the embodied presence behind the screen name as a value to wider society.[3] Suddenly people were being held accountable to the lives they were living both online and offline.

The masks we wear online these days are easily called out by those who know us IRL or those who can search for us by IP address. Our online selves are liable for more than we ever have been before. The responsibility bestowed on today's youth is now akin to growing up as a child star, and even with only thirty-five Facebook friends and an auto-generated Twitter handle, the pressure to perform is great. The masks we choose to wear no longer disguise us but instead filter us into a reconstruction not entirely beyond recognition but perhaps just beyond reality. At what point does the "reality" of our online selves render our true selves worthless? If we can feel good about ourselves only as the people we are on Facebook (filtered, curated, "liked"), we lose touch with the awe-inspiring beauty of human life itself.

The experience of our flesh—underneath which we are "a soul at work"[4]—is, at its core, the only garment of identity we ought to put on (Gen. 3:21). If we model ourselves after Christ and live as followers of the One both divine and human, we are active in what Augustine calls "the great swap" in which Christ took on our flesh that we might receive his spirit.[5] The façade required by the world around us is not required by God. To live as disciples of Jesus is to accept our identity as both children of the divine and recipients of the gift of a human experience. To shy away from either of these in pursuit of anonymity or acceptance is a refusal to embody our true and inherited identity as beloved.

Yet our identities as individuals in this show-and-tell culture are encouraged to be much more than this. Ask any fifteen-year-old social media aficionado to describe their personal aesthetic and they may well present you with nothing short of a branding document, complete with color swatches, lightroom settings, top-performing hashtags, and a font manual. The mask might be what we wear in person, but online we're nothing short of in drag. The exploration of self-expression that the technology of today enables is something to be celebrated—that is, if the result is an ever-expansive love of one's neighbor.

In his 1968 postapocalyptic novel, *Do Androids Dream of Electric Sheep?*, science fiction prophet Philip K. Dick explores the tension of this future reality. The majority of earth's animals have become extinct in the radioactive aftermath of a world war, and owning animals has become the ultimate status symbol. The production and acquisition of lifelike android animals for the sake of keeping up with the Joneses is commonplace, and whether one's animals are real or robotic is the usually unasked question. "Nothing could be more impolite," says the main character. "To say, 'is your sheep genuine?' would be a worse breach of manners than to inquire whether a citizen's teeth, hair, or internal organs would test out authentic."[6]

Fifty years later, to ask if people's social media life is an honest representation of themselves is to suggest their intentionally curated collection of snapshots is not good enough, despite the effort to belong. The standards we feel the need to live up to exist only because of our encounters with the curated world of social media. What was created as a form of personal expression and connection has drawn us farther away from ourselves and one another.

But what if we trusted that we are intimately known? Being freed from the botched narrative we have written for ourselves could liberate us to use our social media in a whole new way. In his article "Digital Privacy: A Squandered Gift," Eric Stoddard argues: "If we assume that God has perfect knowledge of us down to the most mundane and most intimate detail, privacy could easily be evacuated of meaning."[7] What would our feeds look like if we weren't trying to construct or maintain a certain appearance but were trying to faithfully serve by openly witnessing to one another? Casting aside the idea of privacy as we might understand it from the most recent email or WikiLeaks scandal and trusting that our deepest vulnerabilities are already known might free us into a less encumbered form of service. One through which we, too, can be served.

During the writing of this book in mid-2020, America was suffering from yet another horrific display of white supremacy as news of the murder of George Floyd, an African American man suffocated by a white police officer, was plastered over all media platforms. Floyd's death rocked the world. *This* happened, again. People took to social media in the days to follow not to share their own lives but to bring notice to his. #SayHisName began trending, as it had in the wake of so many wrongful deaths of people of color. Public figures, pastors, teachers, artists, politicians, activists, and everyday citizens took the day away from posting personal anecdotes and images and instead shared images of George Floyd, moments of his life, and, most hauntingly, some of his last words: "I can't breathe."[8] On May 26, 2020, the world saw George Floyd. On May 25, 2020, it did not.

Into this place the church can speak. Jesus asks his disciples whether God will not grant justice to those who cry out day and night (Luke 18:7). How might we use digital tools to witness, to affect change? And what might be the result? Henri Nouwen speaks of forming community as impossible if we are filled with either self-rejection or arrogance, two things he argues we are all filled with, especially here, especially now.[9] The practice of shedding this darkness, as Nouwen calls it, is the work of becoming the beloved. It beckons us to ask of ourselves the hardest question: Exactly who do I want to be?

———————

One of the moments that launched this book was an encounter with this kind of question. A middle-aged pastor attending the same workshop as Jason and me was concerned about the optics and boundaries of using social media both personally and professionally. He asked a question that any social media–using pastor has had to consider at one point or another: Should I have a separate personal account from my work account?

All of our better instincts say yes. Social media blurs boundaries in a way our offices and bedrooms do not. There is no closing the door on technology. The ping of a notification draws your attention and before a moment of thought goes into it, a pastoral conversation is taking place, at 11:00 p.m. in your direct messages, you in bed beside your spouse, ready for intimacy (of another sort) moments before but now a debrief (of another sort). The online office hours are 24/7 if we aren't careful. Read receipts alert our followers when we have seen (and ignored) one of their messages. Records of communication are less formal with colleagues and congregants alike. Wouldn't it be easier if we kept our ministerial life and our home life apart? We'll look at the optics of fostering pastoral identity online in the next chapter, but for the average person sitting in the pews (or behind the screen) a work/life identity online is not one that is separate anymore.

———————

This conversation comes up differently in groups of young adults than it does among those who began using social media later in life. In a crowd of Gen Y's, it is common to hear someone joking about the amount of money they would pay for someone to wipe a life on the internet clean from all existence.[10] This is not to say there is a hidden identity you might discover, but it is a reminder that people have grown up in this digital place—the awkward coming-into-the-self we all experience exposed forever for everyone to see. These are normal growing pains but when put on public platforms, our human experiences risk being given the power to shame us into following the wrong prophet (capitalism, popular culture, the bling of a notification).

Becoming the beloved in such an environment means thinking twice before sharing things on social media; consciously looking for an invitation to go deeper with the other and see them for who they are; and risking the FOMO, the YOLO, the MIA because what is more important is this moment and your own experience of it, not how the world sees you experiencing it. Discerning one's life while on display is a great challenge, the most painful growth spurt of them all.

ACRONYMS

ASL:	Age, Sex, Location (a popular identifier in online chatrooms)
ASAP:	As Soon as Possible
MIA:	Missing in Action
BRB:	Be Right Back
FOMO:	Fear of Missing Out
YOLO:	You Only Live Once
IRL:	In Real Life
IP:	Internet Protocol
TMI:	Too Much Information

Into this place the church can speak. Jesus bestows on us power and authority to be teachers wherever we go (Luke 9:1–6). Through approaching our media platforms with Christian charity and an openness toward the journeys of others, we empower those we serve to not only overcome their own faith detours but also embolden others on their own paths. We become sent disciples here, just as we become ourselves.

Perhaps you have had the experience of unintentionally becoming the recipient of someone's social media confession. Without warning, as you have been scrolling through your homepage, you stumble upon a cry for forgiveness. Someone you follow has announced a negligence that landed their child in the hospital or perhaps has laid bare that they have been drinking too much and have decided to stop. The practice of confession is one deeply embedded in our faith. To lay the burden of our sins at the feet of Jesus and be welcomed home, and sent out anew, is the grace that saves. The need for such a practice is obvious in current culture as people immersed in the superficial work of perfection suffer exhaustion. So here it happens.

The challenge in a secular setting, however, is the danger that the confessor's relief of guilt by way of public confession might have the psychosomatic effect of pardon by God. For Dietrich Bonhoeffer, the one with ears to hear the confession must stand in the place of the church, in place of the Christ, in order that the body be restored.[11]

That leaves us, the everyday users of social media, to fulfill that role; the Gen Z, the Millennial, the Boomer. It is a call to pastor unlike ever before—to step into our own authority as bearers of the light, ones oriented always to the good news.

Imagine, in all the seasons of your formation, being consciously and consistently reminded that the water has washed us clean. Even on Instagram.

———————

For someone who comes to social media later in life, the conversation happens differently still. Perhaps you were already a pastor or a leader by the time Facebook became widely used and never had the experience of painstakingly combing through posts to remove all of the red-faced pictures and childhood nicknames. What exists online, then, is the expression of yourself that you grew into, not the growing pains themselves.

Into this place the church can speak. Christ has set us an example that pushes us forward into the world as ones who have been changed (John 13:15). To share these moments of transformation with others is our assignment as Christians.

Throughout the editorial process, Jason and I have reflected on a particular story from the writing of this book. While unintentionally multitasking on an out-of-town work trip, Jason found himself in the middle of a Twitter tit-for-tat with a public theologian. What started as a generic social media engagement quickly turned into a disagreement and eventually, insult. The exchange was public, and for at least one of the parties (though we can assume, to some extent, both) uncomfortable. A later phone call between the two of us revealed very different perceptions of the experience. For Jason, the experience was a public display of being less-than, messy in some way, uncouth. For myself, a follower on the sidelines, the experience was a testimony to the human possibility of our platforms: spiritual authority or otherwise, engaging in the work of our lives is messy.

No public reconciliation took place, despite the consideration of how it might, in an ideal world. What we can encourage as the church is not what is necessarily happening but what we hope to grow into as we ourselves work to become.

I (Jason) was at a nice dinner out of town with friends and professional colleagues—the sort of dinner where you stand to learn something, connect to someone new, and enjoy all at once. These don't come along often. Enjoy them.

No one but myself made me check my Twitter feed. It had blown up. I had earlier posted a conservative-ish sounding quote from an Anglican friend that many had liked, a few quibbled with. But now a Twitter luminary with roughly twenty-five times my followers had retweeted it in a flash of rage. Surely this was untrue, they said. It borrows a conservative trope that has been harmful, they continued. Read their book to see why it was wrong. Naturally my mind left the table, the friends old and new, and went global. The world could see them writing this about me, not trusting me, pillorying me, belittling me, in order to sell their product.

How would I respond?

I tried humor. It didn't mollify the anxiety. I yelled back. Didn't help. They just yelled louder. They took a victory lap at my expense, dispatching me with a witty zinger polished at hosts of speaking events when anyone a smidge to their right had objected at all. I retorted with a much less witty (but much more correct) riposte. And then the dust settled. That was it. The sky didn't fall. No one weighed in on our unpleasant exchange. My dinner had been ruined. Maybe theirs had, though I admired the skill with which they purloined it for marketing purposes. No one was edified. All the decades of education and writing they and I have put in devolved into a schoolyard hissy fit. I'm still embarrassed about it.

I felt exposed, mocked, humiliated. I'm a professional commentator on matters religious and political, and here someone vastly more accomplished than I at playing the celebrity did so at my expense, stepping on my face to vault into a public push for their own product. Admittedly, I felt a touch of pride. Someone famous was tweeting about me. It turned to horror. They're doing it in a way that makes me look like a drooling idiot. I took up arms: I won't let this happen unchallenged! I was vanquished. They're better at the tweetable insult. And then we're done. I felt a touch of what bullied middle schoolers must feel. One of the cool kids is paying attention to me! Oh God, this is the wrong kind of attention. Stand up for yourself! No, disappear. Go away, far away, where they can't hurt you.

The problem here is directly related to social media. They created a caricature of me, lanced it like a boil, and then threw up their arms, glorious in victory. What I actually think is much more nuanced than even what I tweeted. But the medium does not like nuance. It likes hot takes and conflict. I presented a two-dimensional portrait of myself. They demolished that portrait. Something in the actual, three-dimensional me felt demolished too. Anyone who has ever taken the microphone in public knows something of this fear. Sometimes it's even realized. In person, we have three-dimensional selves to deal with. We can still be cruel and condescending, no doubt. But that cruel and condescending part of us is magnified on the socials. It's us, but a worse us.

Can you see why I'm sympathetic with those who denounce the socials, the internet, technology in general? It all makes us little trolls, little bullies, little voyeurs, little President Trumps, rage tweeting at windmills. Burn it all down.

Ooh, wait, someone just tweeted @ me. Maybe this one will be full of kindness, wisdom, and common sense, despite all previous experience and evidence to the contrary . . .

––––––––––––––

Even still, there are people who are only just beginning to use social media. The future of today's youth is as of yet unstained by the humiliation of a tag gone wrong, an opinion un-finessed, or a private moment made public by someone else.

Into this place the church can speak. Jesus asks of us our hardened hearts, attuned neither to God nor to one another (Mark 6:52; 8:17; 10:5), and invites us into the softening that allows us to see one another with generosity and compassion.

Digital literacy classes are now being offered in public schools to help encourage IT proficiency and appropriate critical thinking in online spaces.[12] In addition to computer basics such as typing and rudimentary programming, these classes teach the dangers of neglecting to care about privacy. They also encourage teens to think about what future employers or college admissions advisors might assume based on an online profile. They warn of information silos—the algorithms that only show us more of what we like to look at. But digital literacy is so much more than a lesson in how to safely and effectively use today's technology. It is, as CEO of Affectiva and artificial emotional intelligence pioneer Rana el Kaliouby says, to "enable human beings to retain our humanity when we are in the cyber world."[13]

At its core, the use of our social technologies today inspires a question of ontology: What is real? As Christians, we answer this in relationship to our experiences of God in the world showing us what is true. When we use the tools we have created for justice and reconciliation, for liberation and prophecy, for proclamation and relationship, we are in less danger of being swept away by the artificial lure of distraction versus discipleship. When our lives are integrated, the digital with the physical, we can serve in all places.

To assume the identity of the beloved in a world of faux belonging is to integrate the work of our souls with the masks of our bodies and to share the journey as testimony through whatever means possible, including popular technology. We are called to witness with our lives, and the practice of that witness occurs in every post, every status, every tweet, every like, and every follow. Private or public, if our overarching narrative of the self is one in which we are God's, then the platforms that require us to assume labels and status become redundant.

With the ability now to create entire identities that do not necessarily reflect our non-virtual reality, the distinctions between public and private, embodied and disembodied, real and constructed are increasingly difficult. Whether intentional or not, the core values of our selves cross the border between public and private every time we log on and click "like."

Into this place the church can speak. The disciples ask Jesus, "Teacher, which commandment in the law is the greatest?" and Jesus responds that to love God and neighbor is all we need to remember (Matt. 22:36–40). A friend often uses the example of his marriage when asked about public perceptions of his faith. "If you have known me or followed me (online) for a little while and you haven't realized I have a wife, that might be an indication I'm not valuing that relationship as much as I should be." The same goes for God. If our feeds and our stories aren't sharing our love for God and one another, it might be time to ask some hard questions.

There is an invitation brewing to a form of discipleship unlike any we have encountered. The spectators in this virtual place are less-than generous. "Show us your sheep!" they shout, à la Android. Or, "Is not this the carpenter's son? Is not his mother called Mary?"

(Matt. 13:55). The self-exploration and identity-discovering work of building and tearing down different kinds of selves, the trying on of different masks, is critical. As we compare ourselves each day to the masked and filtered lives of hundreds of friends and strangers alike, it is necessary that we root ourselves in a clear theology of identity while also utilizing the relevant technology to help us live into our identity as disciples of the One in whom we are baptized to belong. The One who was, indeed, both Mary's son and also the Son of God.

Into ourselves and these places, we grow. When we view the different embodiments of our existence in today's society, modern religion and spiritual practice would have us believe our action as people of faith belongs more in one than the other. But if, as Paul suggests, God is working in all things (Rom. 8:28), we cannot remove the technologies of today from this announcement.

The work of Paul Tillich on the Holy Spirit's infiltration of the secular is one such invitation to see the two-dimensional medium of the internet as something more than just a playground for heathens.[14] I bring up Tillich here not to spite my coauthor, who wrongly thought Tillich's day was over, but to offer a perspective that might just set the Spirit loose for you as it did for me. For Tillich, the Spiritual Presence is working with or without us to create Spiritual communities, unaffiliated with the institutionalized church but committed to an eschatological vision of a new way of life.[15] Tillich separates the human spirit (our own intentions) from the divine Spirit (God's intentions) but sees them as greeting each other in bursts of holy intervention that might, for the sake of argument, inspire someone to create a digital community of people committed to serving and showing up for their neighborhood. Christ is not always named on the web, but surely he is not absent.

What might it mean to encounter a community of people online who are not concerned with calling out or influencing but instead busied with the work of welcoming and noticing? Why is the church not already here? Must we wait for another lynching, another trial, another injustice to clearly see those in our midst as others who are beloved?

Each of us in our own bodies is pressing into society and culture, shaping a personal narrative, in order that we might be noticed. Rowan Williams identifies the individual in this way, writing, "I am because I am seen."[16] Yet online it appears the call is only to blend in. A collage of ranunculus, motivational quotes and the expected spattering of happy family-vacation photos create a perfect camouflage, ensuring the masks we wear remain on and the selves we long to share remain isolated.

There is an invitation in our midst and in our ministries to greet God once more where the holy meets the profane—to step into a space covered in filth and to declare it sacred ground. Social media is a place of profound loneliness and yet leaders in our church seem reluctant to climb into the pen. Behind the mask of a congregation, media team, or policy board, a wading is taking place, but there is no full immersion into the muddy world that many of our congregants (or at least future congregants) inhabit full-time. We type our own sermons in the safety of quotation marks and accept friend requests knowing we don't update our Facebook much anyway, instead of trusting ourselves to testify to the call of what it means to follow Jesus, in whom we are who we are.

Social media is not something the church has done particularly well. It is all too often boring, ugly, careful, and desperate. *Come to our Bible study! We still use Comic Sans!* Alternatively, as the pendulum swings, it can become superficial, loud, and presumptuous. *Content won't make you content! Christ will!* You know who you are. Yes, we are all sinners, indeed. But we are called to be different, as disciples and teachers, in this place. We are not here to build a following; we are here to build relationships in the name of the One we follow. The way we begin is by opening our eyes to the world around us—the desperate, presumptuous, hurting world around us that cries out to be seen and loved.

There is a call for authentic displays of discipleship in the world. What does it look like to have faith in the face of life-altering news (a Christian woman I follow on Twitter who lost her husband in a tragically unexpected circumstance tweeted recently, "Lots of my prayers this year have been 'WTF God???'"),[17] to discern God's voice, to make the selfless choice in a self-centered circle? What does it feel like to sit with the suffering when you don't know what to say? How do we celebrate someone else's joy when we don't feel we have been given the same lot of blessings? Why should we give up the luxuries our culture informs us are valuable if we've worked hard our entire lives to attain them?

These are not questions coming only from our Christian brothers and sisters; they are questions arising from the fingertips of our global online community of more than 3.4 billion people,[18] and they are being asked through the desire to be in constant communion with one another. To view social media platforms as shallow, inconsequential, fake, or worse, *private*, is to ignore those citing this as their primary form of self-expression and connection,[19] authentic or otherwise.

We avoid this form of connection in the church because it is work and because it is rough. A computer engineer who has given generously of his time to coach the local church in online security has a response to the complaint about the amount of work it takes to put something online properly: "Security is the enemy of convenience." Part of existing as the church online involves creating a sanctuary for people, in all stages of their online identity, that protects them from a world constantly working to divide our sense of self in an unhelpful way. It takes little effort to put some form of ourselves online these days, but it takes a commitment to the landscape to integrate our whole selves in a way that liberates us from the constraints of perceived personal and public disassociation.

We cannot separate the public and the personal anymore, not if we wish to grow deeper with one another. Things might get rough. There is the vulnerable nature of putting ourselves as leaders fully into the sightlines of those who may or may not agree with what we have to say or how we say it. There is the fear that we have little of value to contribute to a platform that already houses so much beauty or, worse, that someone might value our trash so much that it leads them astray. There is the time it takes to craft both thoughtful and thoughtless bites for chewing on and the time it takes to undo the damage when someone forgets we're human and doesn't take what we say with the proverbial grain of salt.

In the time of coronavirus, pastors have begun to experience this sense of vulnerability and exposure like never before. As most of the world was forced to retreat online, those used to giving sermons to intimate groups of fifty were now encountering what it meant to occupy public space, where an audience could easily double or triple and the result could linger in cyberspace forever.

It is interesting that this shift in our way of being has felt less secure than the buildings we have been occupying. The church has always been a public space, open to the work of sheltering vulnerable, unwell, angry, even dangerous individuals. There is no denying, however, that YouTube or Vimeo have never claimed to be sanctuaries. Look at the comment section of any widely viewed worship service and you'll see the hatred that many bring into an environment born for love.

This is our perception of impersonal interaction on the internet. It is a place where those who long to be seen are trampled over and where the loudest, most vicious voices are heard first. But it is not just a perception. Kaliouby identifies this as the result of being "emotion blind." In other words, because our computers can't detect our emotion, when we enter into virtual space, even to be in community, we lose our EQ entirely.[20] Our way of being, however, as those walking into this place with the feet of Christ, is to bring with us the holy water, offering a story of salvation that makes room for the disguises to wash away and, despite the empathic tone-deafness, offers a chance to be transformed.

This is not a fleeting hope. We know this transformation ourselves. The call of a pastor or teacher or guide is not one we accept lightly. As we grow into our roles in the church, we grow into ourselves, learning new ways to see God in the work we do and new ways to be Christlike with the people we encounter. The masks we put on aren't necessarily phony or misleading. Flipping through a book of fairy tales, we encounter this metamorphosis constantly. The Frog Prince, a handsome Beast, Shrek and Fiona (a modern fairy tale, I insist) all tell of a face that was covered in order to return to the true self. Revealing, each in a sparkly conclusion, that who we are is ever changing and that we are worthy as-is. The story is told of a Victorian-era card sharp who is suddenly overcome with love for a virtuous young woman. Abandoning his also less-than-virtuous paramour, he rushes to propose marriage to the angel, but she will only marry one with the face of a saint, not the face of a gambler and a cheat. He repairs to a mask-maker, who fashions him a visage of a saint, which he must wear the rest of his life. Living up to his new face, he returns his ill-gotten gains and swears off gambling. He weds the virtuous young woman. But then the paramour appears to unmask him. When she rips the wax from his face, all are astonished that his face has actually taken on the contours of the mask. Goodness is no mere ruse. Wear it, and it will transform your very face. Max Beerbohm wrote this fantasy as a riposte to Oscar Wilde's *The Picture of Dorian Gray* and called it "The Happy Hypocrite" to indicate that goodness is, in fact, more contagious than villainy.

When we entered these roles (pastor, teacher, friend), we brought with us our whole selves, but we also brought the selves we were not yet sure how we were going to be. The selves who have never comforted a grieving widow or held the hand of a teenage girl trying to decide what to do about her unexpected pregnancy. The selves who have never held a child before, let alone drawn a cross on an infant's forehead as a sign of God's covenant to love and protect them. These were identities we had to assume before we ever became them and in doing so we knew we were following a long line of faithful disciples as they assumed their true identities. To put on the new self is to be sent by Christ (John 20:21), responsively, though not altogether willingly, to places in which we are afraid both to see and to be seen.

To be made in God's image opens up infinite possibilities of self-creation; the selves we are learning to embody online are one part of that faithful project. As any youth minister or parent knows, experimenting with one's voice or appearance, one's friend circle or passions, is part of a process of maturation that brings with it both challenges and victories that affect us and our relationship with God for our entire lives. This turning toward and turning away from the self is a dance that we participate in, constantly feeding the ego by asking, "Who am I?" all the while ignoring the plea of our faith to step into an identity unpulled by the tractor beam of society and instead given meaning by God.

The Spirit is alive here, giving rise to the emotions that set us down one path or another, encouraging relationships, affixing itself to our bodies that we might remember there is more to be than just accepted.

Through all the iterations of ourselves, a blessing is being whispered: *May you know that you are holy. Yes, this one, too, is beloved.*

Who we are, in the age of social media and artificial intelligence, does not need to be any different from who we were before these things began to shape every aspect of our lives. The soul, in other words, is still the soul. Yet there is no denying that we see ourselves differently, constantly being shown a mirror in which we see every evidence of being an imposter, and in which we see all our failures. We are celebrities who never asked for it and certainly have never seen a Kardashian-sized paycheck, and we treat ourselves in the same way. With every glimpse into this mirror we find something else to change, a different thought pattern that hinders our ability to be everything to everyone, and so we create another layer of the self. One that has perhaps mastered the art of political correctness, of biting one's tongue, of pinning down that one baby hair that has never grown more than an inch in all your life.

It is a hard truth to swallow: we are different online than we are in our physical form. I (Andria) am reminded of the time I started a new job as a youth minister and had one of the teenagers say to me, "I follow you on Instagram—I had no idea you would be so low-key awkward in real life!" It is the plexiglass boundary that exists between being vulnerable and being open to voyeurism. We are encouraged to share every ounce of our lives until it no longer serves the us we are trying to project. We might all be exhibitionists now, but is any of it real?

The Christian life isn't a call to be on and off the moral clock. It is a call to marry our public and private selves into a union of unconditional grace that persists into the mess of the world as beloved, aesthetically on point or not. When we ask ourselves, in light of digital technology, "Who am I?" what we are really seeking to know is what sets us apart. Where can I stand out? How can I make myself known? How can I be seen? What is my *thing*?

When we ask the same questions in the light of our faith, what we are longing to understand is what binds us together. Where is my community? Where have I experienced radical welcome? How have I known God's promises of faithfulness?

Into this place the church can speak. Jesus sat at the table with his disciples on the night before his death, sharing wine and sharing bread, making one promise: that they would remember. Not each to himself, but together, for always (Matt. 26:26–29).

Before her tragic passing in early 2019, Christian author and public theologian Rachel Held Evans set one such example of the self online. Her intention was to use social media to bring people together in all their forms of individualism under a gospel of truth and acceptance. One of her many gifts was an authenticity that traversed the boundaries of this online persona and enabled others to connect through her in a more embodied way. When Jason wrote about her death, he encouraged people to look up the (still active) hashtag #Because ofRHE and see for themselves the "vast, digital church she planted, with moving testimonies from those who, through her work, were wooed into following Christ, called into ministry, and summoned from despair into an affirmation of life."[21]

It is amazing how widely we can minister when we stop trying to be anything other than enough. Authenticity and empathy in a space that knows too little of either can bring people together with powerful force.

Connecting through things such as rare diseases, secluded locations, trauma, or marginalized circumstances, entire demographics of people are finding that our online social platforms can in fact genuinely connect us if we aren't afraid to share of ourselves in a way that might not be "mainstream." While the pressure to conform to a certain standard of presentation (all the while remaining "different" or set apart from the crowd) is only becoming more intense, the rate of rejection of this social media model is only growing.

Most digital natives have experimented with stepping away from the platforms entirely. They cite reasons such as feeling overwhelmed, exhausted, depressed, or distracted; experiencing worse health; encountering "fake news"; and being concerned about privacy and failing relationships.[22] They tend to discover a quick fix with as little as thirty days away from screens.[23] Results such as less anxiety, less interrupting ego, less materialistic fixation, and less carpal tunnel syndrome appear without any additional lifestyle changes. People also discover that they have more freedom, more time with friends, more income, more mindfulness, and more joy. These are no small gains and blessed losses. Upon returning to social media (one might ask why), they are encouraged to put new boundaries in place to try to maintain the bliss they found: no phone after 8:00 p.m., no checking Twitter in bed, only an hour a day, promise.

But does the self-imposed moderation diet work? Does it make room for an increased sense of self or for security in the self that is here and now? Perhaps for some, but as Tristan Harris (former Google ethicist turned founder of the Center for Humane Technology) says, we can't solve the downgrading of humankind by simply switching our phones to grayscale and turning off notifications.[24] The fact remains: who we are is adapting to the digital world we live in. Whether a thirteen-year-old is joining Instagram for the first time or a thirty-year-old is rejoining the millions of users after a thirty-day break, presenting ourselves to the masses changes us. We can only hope to remain anchored to something real.

Luckily, there is a widespread longing for this kind of use of our social platforms. For the first decade of its existence it seemed like all there was to encounter were carefully curated feeds of pastel colors, happy children, and professional accomplishments. The idea that someone would intentionally make themselves look messy by presenting a realistic glimpse into their life seemed to be against the entire point. We have, thankfully, seen a cultural shift take place in the rise of dislike for the classic social media–influencer template and in the push for authenticity.[25] Genuine sharing (albeit the occasional overcorrection, #TMI) has been encouraged instead.

The emergence of social media culture has forced us to ask "Who am I?" and to answer only in the language of physical appearance, material wealth, and textbook cleverness (triple threat if you possess all three). This type of social media engagement has drawn us apart from each other and has led us on an exhaustive search for the modern notion of self, turning away from something that has existed all along: the soul. Yet these tools of our time have also extended an invitation into a kind of discipleship that practices what it posts. In a world of billions of followers, who are we as the ones who left our nets at the edge of the sea and committed to walking a different path?

There is no rule stating we must do it right. The Jesus's first disciples themselves could not always agree—or even believe. They went back to those nets a time or two. We cannot possibly respond to every injustice, know what to say in our heartbreak after every disaster, stand in allyship with all the oppressed, or avoid causing offense with the casual post of a personal opinion. Furthermore, it is unnecessary to use social media to showcase how we have successfully done so. What the virtual world needs, if it is to retain its humanity, is to see that the growing pains of a life do not negate one's place in the kingdom. What a blessing it is to have this tool! Millions of people longing to be seen, with profiles marked public, and a church equipped to say to them, "You are beautiful."

If we are ever to become in this world of belonging, we must start right here: baptized into one body by the grace of Jesus Christ, unmasked by the power of the Holy Spirit, and beloved, in all our iterations, for the world to see.

- Have you ever tried on a new self that affected the old (perhaps first a Halloween costume, a uniform, or even an alter ego)? To what self did you return or become?

- What is your first memory of social networks? How much of who you are today was affected by this experience?

- How does it feel when someone suggests you go off-grid for a time? Is this a practice you would revel in or resent?

TWO

A Pastoral Personality

The question that started it all: Should a minister have personal social media accounts?

Honestly, I hope so. Keeping in mind that I (Andria, the digital native) have never *not* had them, I'd like to offer up some models for why it might be valuable to let people see us as we are, both behind and out from behind the pulpit. I'd also like to offer some empathy for the road ahead. A concretely manifest public identity in addition to a secure pastoral one is a relentless undertaking, one that requires constant attention and self-awareness (often when we don't feel like it). There is a difference between the way we use public platforms to share our lives when we are called to be attentive to the lives of others, and it is not as simple as hitting "retweet" and turning off the light. The work of discipling in a context that includes this online space is not just a way of presenting ourselves but a way of ourselves being present. And there is no one right way to do it. To not do it at all, however, won't cut it.

Before clergy had social media it's a wonder anyone ever invited us over for dinner. There is a saying that, just like a doctor, when a pastor enters a room they automatically become the summation of every pastor each individual in that room has ever encountered. The saying exists because the majority of these pastors have been, quite frankly, a disappointment. So, without warning, upon entering a new environment the weight on a pastor's shoulders shifts from that of word, sacrament, and deed to that of systemic racism, abuse of power, sexual misconduct, theological warfare, or whatever the experience of the environment is. To every new person the pastor meets, the pastor is reduced to the worst pastor the person ever encountered.

It is no surprise, then, that Millennial(ish) ministers have taken to social media with gusto; it is a chance to be our own selves in a world of uniformly villainous pastors. We are not all the same! As if growing into one's own identity in the spotlight of the socials wasn't enough to make you cringe, might we submit into evidence exhibit B: Clergy Twitter. Don't worry, though, it gets easier.

Perhaps somewhat concerning, it appears that before priests tweeted, they bottled up all their personal emotions and experiences and hung them up with their albs. Apart from the occasional Sunday confessional from the pulpit, they were not just like us. They were other.

I'm reminded of a story my mother tells at dinner parties to lighten the mood whenever Christian charity is lacking in a conversation around denominational divides. While waiting one day in the checkout line at a grocery store, she noticed the woman in front of her scanning covers of various tabloids, presumably looking for something interesting to fill the ninety seconds of time it would take for the cashier to scan the woman's carton of eggs (pre–cell phones, you see). Eventually a cover piqued the woman's interest enough to pull the magazine off the shelf, and she and my mother read the title at the same time: "My Priest Is the Father of My Baby!" The woman, obviously delighted by the gossip, opened the magazine. My mother, from whom I come by it all quite honestly, snorted and said, "That's funny. So is mine!" The other woman, presumably a Catholic, looked as if she wished to switch registers. My mother, the wife of an Anglican cleric, laughed as she unloaded her eggs. At that moment, to that woman, my father was every priest. "Celibate," but not very good at it, apparently.

My father was certainly not every priest. Now retired, he served as a navigator in the Navy before leaving the military for a seminary degree and a three-point charge. He remained in congregational ministry for more than thirty-five years. There are many things I consider distinctive about him: he is a master wordsmith who never needs notes, a sailor, a woodworker, an avid cyclist, and a motorcycle rider. None of those things compare, however, to who he was to the congregation who, knowing his military background and his affinity for aviation stunts, asked if he would grace them at the first annual church picnic by jumping out of an airplane. My father declined, mumbling something about how one cannot simply jump out of an airplane and into a public park, but the point was made clear: it was necessary for the parish priest to have *a thing*.

The Guardian claimed much the same recently, on a different level, when it published an article with the headline "I Have More Followers than the Church of England" identifying several "religious stars" of Instagram.[1] While the public accountability of clergy has always been a virtue, this is likely not what Paul had in mind when he suggested the priest as an icon (1 Tim. 2:5). To mediate between God and people is not to make of the self an idol (look at me!) but to point to Christ in all one does (look at him!).

The article, however, points to several different religious officials, of differing faith traditions, who have amassed large followings on their Instagram accounts. Each one, it seems, has *a thing*. Be it body art, an affinity for spin classes, a meat-free diet, whiskey, or even—in my father's pre-Instagram case—a parachute, their title was not enough to earn them the ear of the people. There had to be something else. Something more . . . earthly.

A Twitter exchange in early August 2020 between Daniel Brereton (@RevDaniel) and one of his seventy-five thousand followers showcased this in real time. The Toronto priest had received negative feedback on a photo of himself at the gym wearing a tank top, to the tune of "how provocative, how vain, how unchristian."[2] His response, that taking care of himself is a faithful example of healthy living, was met with further backlash for not being pastoral enough. In an email exchange, I asked Brereton about these kinds of interactions, and he responded that in such circumstances it is often a case of people thinking a priest shouldn't do or say something that he has done or said. He often makes a point to follow up with the person and have an exchange about what offended them. Most times it is a case of him not fitting someone else's mold of what a pastor should be.[3] To publicly be the individual and the pastor in all moments and meet all expectations is exhausting. It is also important.

Brereton wrote to me, "I feel very strongly that even as a priest I must be 'myself' and true to who I am. After all, that is who God called into ministry and who the Church ordained." When asked if he consciously changed his social media habits upon entering the ministry, he suggested that his online authenticity has been one of the things that enables people to trust him in his priestly role.[4]

For Jes Kast (@revjeskast), a minister in the United Church of Christ near Penn State University with whom I spoke on Zoom, the cultivation of an authentic social media identity has been a process years in the making, beginning with her handle itself. "My handle sets the tone," she says of her accounts. By identifying herself by her vocation up front, she is held accountable to a different voice. It is distinctly hers (a voice she describes as out, lesbian, ordained, and feminine), but it is also the voice of a woman who holds an immense amount of theological authority. "People know I love red lipstick and gardening, because those things help shape my theological voice, but this isn't about a glorification of me, it is an obligation to humanity."

This obligation to humanity is a refrain that is clear in Kast's personal philosophy of social media: "When we try to totally incarnate ourselves in the moment, that also makes room for others. I think that's gospel," she says. "If I truly believe this story—this good news— then I know that my life is a variation of it, and that creates more room for hope and joy." Joy is something that radiates from Kast, not only in conversation but on her platforms. She cites John 10:10 as a guiding principle: "How does my social media lead to abundant life for me and others?"[5]

For the apostle Paul, the role of pastor is one in which the self very much empties into the image of Christ. Undoubtedly, the evangelist would have been all over Twitter, alternating altar calls with grievances and salutations, but he likely wouldn't have shared an image of his breakfast. It is, after all, not about us (Phil. 2:4). However, we cannot be so quick as to dismiss the self, either. Paul offers us lists of gifts that make up the body of Christ, indicating that the self still has an integral role to play in the work of the pastor who is shaping the church in the world. People like Brereton and Kast are demonstrating with spirit and—dare I say—sass, exactly how integral this embodiment is.

Our own identities as Christians, shaped in part by our cultural context and in part by our faith formation, do matter in the building and planting of the kingdom. Jim Keat, the digital minister for Riverside Church, told me in a conversation (also digitally) that while in seminary, in addition to learning Greek and Hebrew, he also took on learning CSS and HTML because "those languages were only going to become more useful."[6] This kind of personal response to the times and to his own interests has enabled him and the ministry team at Riverside Church to build a community of people around the world who engage in the gospel from wherever they are.

Keat joined social media for curiosity's sake back when Facebook still required people to have a college email address, but he didn't really start engaging in it until doing ministry. It was quickly apparent that these platforms were ones through which communities of all kinds were going to be in relationship with one another.

Keat and his wife have designed a life perfect for social media despite not being overly concerned with their personal use of it. Their family motto, "free and simple," led the couple to work remotely, traveling the country and living in an Airstream. Two weeks before his first child was due, Keat said, "He's already got his own Instagram. A little baby and an Airstream? That's the ultimate clickbait!" Yet the pastoral isn't removed for Keat either, despite having his own travel YouTube channel and the label "Airstream ambassador." "I try to plan some of my travels around where online congregants live so I can meet them when I pass through town," he says.

Speaking with him reminds me of a comment a professor once made, tired of hearing excuses about the discomfort some mainline seminarians have around evangelism. "Live a life so interesting that people have no choice but to ask you what it is you do so differently from everyone else."

From talking with Keat, I can see the difference: his work and his life are bound together by a desire to bring the gospel forward into this time and into tomorrow. Holding this purpose both personally and pastorally he has been able to use the platforms to form authentic relationships. "It shouldn't be a bulletin board," Keat said of Twitter. "Twitter itself is *the thing*." He echoes Gary Vaynerchuk's online approach by saying social media shouldn't just be a broadcast, but a form of engagement.[7] If we are using social media as a form of annunciation but neglecting the reciprocity or relational potential, we aren't doing it right.

For Keat, this is the primary place where his pastoral use of social media takes over. "I'll experiment on my own accounts and see what gets traction—that's how I know what the church should implement." The question that arises next, he says, is, "Who should tweet this? Me, or Riverside?" When asked how he decides, he surprises: he can be more risky as Riverside than he can as himself. Riverside stresses that they are an "interdenominational, interracial, international, open, welcoming, and affirming church and congregation," whereas Keat recognizes himself within those identifiers as a "straight cis white guy." Speaking boldly about the ways of Jesus as the church, and having an opportunity to engage others in what it looks like to disciple alongside them, is more important than expressing his own opinions.

For those who haven't been experimenting with HTML since seminary, however, this kind of digital integration and fluency is complicated. Some days it feels as if it is not enough to live a remarkable life if we are not seen doing so.

During the early months of the global pandemic of 2020–21, the most vocal concern heard by pastors around the country was that of comparison—when we can see how others are doing it, we question our own ways. Social media is good at provoking this, and comparison has always been the thief of joy. Because the nature of the pandemic has meant our churches have shifted to worshiping online, congregations and their leadership have been more visible to colleagues than ever before. Pastors traded Netflix for church, binge-watching services around the world because for the first time they could—and perhaps they wanted to—see if they were keeping up.

For those unfamiliar with the technicalities of worshiping and serving online, the prospect of starting from scratch in the span of a week or two was deeply distressing. This concern was made more prominent by watching, every second of every day, as colleagues managed to pull off something brilliant.

Many congregations in rural areas, equipped with one, maybe two, ministry staff, looked at urban churches with endowment funds and multimembered staff teams as exemplars of what steps they *should* be taking in the midst of crisis: a Sunday service, a separate children's program, online youth group, online small group ministry, a coffee hour, and a new Bible study titled "Living in a Liminal Time" seemed mandatory. What were pastors doing with their time if not these things? The public perception of what church should look like in such a time as this weighed heavily on those already serving with both hands.

Filled with guilt, resentment, and defensiveness, there was nothing left in the cup to overflow. Between managing the pastoral needs of a congregation in the midst of collective trauma, managing one's own boundaries and spiritual self-care, and fulfilling the duties always required by a role with public responsibility, appearing behind is enough to make one feel negligent and incapable. It comes as no shock to learn the famous quote "comparison is the thief of joy" has been for years misattributed to everyone from Roosevelt to Kierkegaard when it was (so they say) coined by a nineteenth-century Scottish preacher. We are a susceptible kind.

Yet we are each called, through those Pauline gifts of the Spirit, to work in this church in this time, in our own way. It is not for each of us to do it all, but for each of us to respond faithfully to our own communities. Social media does not show us what faithful looks like in every circumstance. It shows us the algorithmic definition of faithful: bright, bubbly, and production-passionate. Such a response is not the whole story.

During the pandemic, we quickly saw the communities who had on their ministry teams those gifted with leadership, prophecy, and teaching. Springing forth from their corners of the internet were responsive sermons, astutely themed conversation series, commitments to programming, webinars for other church leaders, and new virtual platforms to manage it all. These are gifts the church cannot exist without (1 Cor. 12), but they are not the only gifts. These are not the gifts that would deliver water or medicine or toilet paper to a couple in their eighties who were too afraid to leave the house.

Thomas Irby, a United Methodist pastor in Tacoma, Washington, was unfussed by all this pressure as his state led the charge on lockdowns after a coronavirus outbreak in a care facility forty-two miles north of his congregation. Now someone I consider to be a Twitter friend, Irby spoke with me over FaceTime about the changes in church when COVID-19 was first developing. When asked about the most surprising request to come from his congregation in the online-only times, he responded not with a resounding cry for digital programming but instead recalled that several of his elderly congregants asked him for distilled water, as they were unable to get to the store and needed the filtered water for their CPAP machines. In a world paralyzed by a virus that robs people of their breath, he could provide something that would help his people catch theirs.[8]

Being attuned to the needs of our neighbor requires neither the resources of a television studio nor the expertise of George Lucas. Better news yet, responding to these needs doesn't require these either. Mother Teresa is thought to have said, "We cannot all do great things. But we can do small things with great love." We are desperate for people who pastor like that.

Over one hundred years ago, in 1918, First Methodist Church in Tacoma closed its doors to worship and opened them to the sick and dying as the Spanish Flu swept through the city, filling hospitals beyond capacity.[9] Irby's COVID-19 response has precedent in a church that has long sought to love their neighbors. While Irby's church, Mason United Methodist, is worshiping online using Facebook Live to keep congregants connected, Irby's call was not first to launch a year's worth of online programming but instead to love with small gestures those he had been called to serve.

Encountering one another online is one of the gifts this digital technology has to offer us. Instead of being pressured to perform differently or to produce constantly, we can use these tools to their maximum potential and to their greatest good—to share. In the breaking of the bread we remember the body of Christ as it is made up of each of us. Individual, but not alone. Or—to reiterate our COVID-19 language—together, apart.

In serving the church as pastor, Richard Niebuhr commends a deep understanding of the current cultural environment. The pastor's identity is therefore faithful to the pulse of the Spirit and to the continuously shifting culture it inhabits.[10] While for some this can look like using technology to hear the needs of the people, for others (for many) it can look like inhabiting technology to provide what the people might need to hear.

For Irby, the best approach is a both/and. Because the people in his congregation are not the same thousand people who follow him on Twitter, the ministry is different. One environment requires a form of servanthood while the other allows for a freedom of leadership and influence that might draw in those from other demographics. He writes, "A lot of people are connecting with our church because of how I use Twitter." He speaks of his engagement with the Black Lives Matter movement in the wake of the 2020 protests in Seattle and around the world and how the content he posts online has drawn multiple Antifa folks toward his church. "The story is similar for all of them: 'I grew up Christian but never found a church that embraced radical politics. I want to see what's happening at your church!'"[11]

In the pastor's ability to exist in this changing and volatile space, many people are finding a door creaking open to Christianity again where it had once closed for them. An email came in recently asking about online membership in a church not only in a different town but in a different country, because his town had no progressive worshiping community. He had been watching my social media pages and thought he and his family might find a deeper sense of community in the church I worked for. Without social media, he was left feeling unsafe and unsupported in his faith journey. With it, he was invited into a deeper conversation about how following Christ is still possible in the midst of religious trauma.

When asked about the spirited state of his personal social media versus the perfunctory state of his church's feeds in a conversation with Jason and me, Rich Villodas (@richvillodas) of New Life Fellowship in New York City revealed a slightly different approach from Jim Keat. Whereas Keat filters his social media posts based on content and voice between church and self, Villodas responded that as the pastor, his responsibility is to preach with his life to those who might encounter him, not the organization of the church he serves. This assumption of responsibility is one that enhances the pressure on the pastor but also responds to the embedded understanding of distance between the ordained minister and the laity. Both ministers do not need to be separated from themselves to point toward Jesus.

Jes Kast echoes this in her sentiment of obligation to humanity. She calls her social media posts "testimony," and while her personal platforms have certainly drawn people to Faith UCC, she makes it clear that discipleship within the community is a priority. "When I'm called from this place," she says, "I want to make sure the people who came for me stay for [the church]."[12]

The responsibility of testifying tirelessly in bite-sized chunks for all the world to see and hear (and critique) is not one that is listed in our job descriptions. Concerns rightfully come up when considering boundaries and capacity. *If I can be seen and reached everywhere, at all times, I won't ever be able to shut off.* Part of maintaining a posture of joy in times like this is knowing when using social media is not enjoyable. For Kast, this is a constant question, in partnership with firm boundaries. She has recently employed a practice of a weekly digital sabbath, and she confesses to not being afraid of blocking those who degrade her or the community she loves (a "block ministry," she calls it). But Kast also recognizes that through the noise often come genuine connection and requests for support and guidance. It is here that her handle holds her accountable to the purpose of her accounts.

"I'm very thoughtful about how I post—even about the snarky stuff!—because I need to have the mental state to attend to it afterward." Attending to the rubble is what sets the pastor on the platform apart from the parishioner.

In some ways, this is the return of the age-old question: Would you wear your clerical collar on the plane? Are we prepared to manage the engagement that comes from showing up and preaching with our whole lives?

The kenotic framework of our call is at once selfless and self-demanding. To empty ourselves entirely of ego and personal longing in order to leave abundant space only for the divine is a call unlike any other. We must know ourselves, enjoy ourselves, be ourselves in order that we listen to, delight in, and imitate Christ. While we are not ever asked to forego the moments of joy that come (when we are not busy comparing ourselves to others), it is expected that all our joy, all our praise, and all our being is given over to Jesus through our following.

If we ever hope to turn our pastoring off, perhaps what Thomas à Kempis writes in *The Imitation of Christ* is correct: to be unknown and unregarded is the only way to learn or know anything.[13] But in a world where who we are seems to be what people see of us, we have an opportunity to share our gifts with the world as part of living well. To be Christlike in this place we must not set ourselves above but set ourselves apart. Here to bless in word, sacrament, and deed so that through Christ all those who follow are, too, in possession of *a thing* that sets them apart.

- If someone were to identify you by *a thing* outside of your vocation, what would it be? How could this part of you be of service in your ministry?

- If you had a personal online "philosophy," what might it be? What would your church's be?

- In a world that most notably recognizes charismatic leaders and shiny platforms, how do we give ourselves over to the small gestures—the ones that change a life, not only influence it?

THREE

The Opposite of Technology

There is an old preacher's saw about the Tower of Babel and the miracle of Pentecost. I (Jason) have heard sermons that claim this; I've even preached a few: Pentecost undoes Babel. Pay attention to preachers' saws. Sometimes they show how lazy we preachers are, rehashing rather than studying for fresh illumination. But sometimes these saws linger because they tell truths.

First edge of the saw: the Tower of Babel is about human presumption, the ego to build empires, which God detests. "Come, . . . let us make a name for ourselves; otherwise we shall be scattered abroad" (Gen. 11:4). They build a tower up to the heavens, making it out of thoroughly baked bricks, held together with mortar and stone (11:3). The tower is impressive, meant to be a lasting monument, so high we have to crane our necks to see it. Note: this is a communal effort. Sometimes, in our efforts to undo individualism, we speak as though "community" is the positive answer to everything. Here a community sets about its idolatrous self-establishment together.

Yet God is unimpressed. The Lord still has to "come down" to see this tower. The best human efforts to make ourselves eternal produce a pathetic monument that the Lord still has to squint to see. You might read Genesis 11:6, "this is only the beginning of what they will do," as divine hand-wringing that humanity will be able to accomplish anything. Yet God scatters their speech and their effort without difficulty (11:7). As ever with God, divine "punishment" is also divine grace—being scattered across the face of the earth is humanity's vocation from the beginning. We are to go, be fruitful and multiply, and bless others (Gen. 1:28). God only has one way to be—loving. That way is sometimes experienced as punishment, sometimes as grace, but it is all altogether God. When we are seeking to establish ourselves, God's punishment/grace is to scatter us. In those moments, however high we build our towers, the heavenly court has to break out the microscope to see us, has to go out of its way to become small enough to confuse us.

The Tower of Babel is clearly an origin story. Like other legends, it is trying to explain something. Who are our Babylonian enemies? Well, let me tell you a story. Why are there so many languages on earth, and why are we so incapable of communicating across cultures? Here's a story about that. More to the point now: Why are we human beings always trying to build lasting monuments to ourselves, to establish our permanence and our dominance? And why does it never work, even as we get better and better at building towers that vainly seek eternity?

Well, let me tell you a story.

The disciples of Jesus are all together in one hidden room. I should say erstwhile, former disciples. Jesus is gone. They were never *good* disciples—always misunderstanding and then betraying and abandoning. But then a hurricane comes. Tongues of fire rain down. New languages fill their mouths. The Holy Spirit is pouring out wind and fire and language. Disciples who had been far from God even when Christ was near are becoming full of God now that the Spirit is near.

Their fellow Jews overhear them. They are pilgrims in Jerusalem for the festival of Pentecost and hear these Galileans speaking in *their* languages. The miracle is one of communication. The Tower's reversal is being reversed. Amazed and astonished, the overhearers recite (apparently in unison) their nationalities: they are Parthians, Medes, Elamites, residents of Mesopotamia, Judea, Cappadocia, Pontus, Asia, Phrygia, Pamphylia, Egypt, Cyrene Libya, Rome, Cretans and Arabs, Jews and proselytes, yet "in our own languages we hear them speaking about God's deeds of power" (Acts 2:11). Some scoff. They are drunk. Peter clarifies: it is only 9:00 a.m. There's time for the bar later. And he stands and gives the first Christian sermon, the first speech anointed by the Spirit's fire and wind and language. The resurrection is the culmination of history. God is stitching back together the fabric of humanity, which we have torn. Repent and believe the good news. They do. Three thousand of them. But they don't stay and build the first megachurch of Jerusalem. That would be Babel's logic. They go home, scattering to all the points on the compass, starting countless mini-churches, telling of God's deeds of power in their own languages and in their own communities.[1]

Babel is about the wonder of human ingenuity. We really can build amazing towers. The problem is that we think these deliver us immortality, an eternal claim on a spot of land, the "freedom" to be heedless of God's story or commands. It is not ingenuity that is condemned. The same sort of massive building project was divinely commanded and blessed in the story of Noah. Creation got a fresh start, with two of every single animal, humans included, when Noah, God's favored, built a boat massive enough to contain the world. Building is not the problem. Building heedless of God's direction, in a way that claims to offer insurance against divine whims, is futile. Viewed from one angle, Babel's tower makes great sense. Build 'em if you got 'em. Viewed from a similar angle, Noah's boat looks like a boondoggle. God's story will make you avoid things that look sensible, and do things that look absurd. The calling and gifts of human dexterity and resourcefulness are not the problem. Babel's imagination is the problem. What is the solution?

Pentecost. Here is a miracle, a mystery, a birth no one could have conceived, yet after its appearance in history, none of us could unimagine it. God does a miracle that requires no more human initiative than what it takes to slink off to a hidden room, defeated together. There is a profusion of images, a deluge on the senses, a flood of wind and fire and words (no water this time—God promised, remember the rainbow? [Gen. 9:8–17]). But God doesn't build a new Babel. Specific cultures and languages are honored with God's words, not flattened into monochrome similitude. God scatters the people with grace/punishment. These Jews and proselytes from all over the world return home from their pilgrimage with quite a story. Most dismiss it as drunkenness. Some turn over their lives to this new form of intoxication. And a church that delights in difference, in the local, in going and telling, is born.

Insofar as technology pulls us away from the local and the particular, it is a trap to be avoided. But can we trick it, rewire it, to make us attend more deeply to the local, the particular, even the sacramental?

We might think of sacraments as the opposite of technology (we will deal with the question of online Communion specifically in chap. 7). Technology has taught us to be impatient in new ways. Why won't this device work? Where can I get a better signal? What's wrong with this thing? One hallmark of the device paradigm, Albert Borgmann says, is that we can't understand how a device works, nor can we repair it—it takes some sort of specialist or, in consumerist culture, it's cheaper to throw it away and get a new one.[2] The mechanics are opaque to most of us. In the church's sacraments, however, a miracle occurs. God is present among us in a fresh way, to save. Sacraments require the invocation of the hurricane-force, fiery Holy Spirit. No Spirit, no Eucharist, and no baptism. The church has worked hard to minimize the requirements for a valid sacrament. Be baptized by water in the name of the Father, the Son, and the Holy Spirit, and you're good. Receive bread and wine, blessed and broken and shared, and Jesus is right there among us. Or maybe better, we're right there with him, in the upper room, awaiting the Passover of the Lord. The number of things required for the sacrament to "work" is as few as possible. No need to bang on the thing in frustration: Why won't this work?! Of course, we cannot *prove* that a sacrament has worked. We can only rarely feel the hurricane, see the tongues of flame, heed the languages, feel the heat. We must trust that the God who is always saving is here and working anew by the power of the Spirit.

Longtime experts in prayer suggest that God often withholds comforting manifestations, especially as we grow in maturity—such props and fortifications should no longer be needed. With technology, the logic is opaque, the outcome unsure, the result glitzy if success comes (call a repair guy if not).[3] With a sacrament, the logic is clear, the outcome trustworthy, the result thoroughly unglamorous, and the charge is to press on, especially when we are long without evidence of efficacy. How do we know if a sacrament "works"? A lifetime of cross-bearing, growing in the likeness of Christ, becoming friends with all of Jesus's weird friends, the kingdom dawning.

Preachers' saws can make you lazy. Babel's destruction is not undone, the tower is not rebuilt, at Pentecost. The church's Pentecostal explosion regards the specific, delights in the telling of God's deeds of power in every human language. This happens often in history since we have built bigger and better Babels. They will not last, any more than the first tower did. They look strong, but they're actually weak. The church of many languages scatters, getting progressively smaller as it radiates out from Jerusalem. It looks weak, but it is actually remarkably strong. God's grace/punishment makes us a going-and-telling multilingual miracle-dependent people. Human invention will be involved. But we did not invent this story, and we do not establish it.

The church has a story for human efforts to establish ourselves: Babel. And we have a description for God's work to regard the local, to love the specific face of the other, even to learn the other's language (slowly, painstakingly) to tell of God's deeds of power: Pentecost.

It is not hard to find theologians condemning the place of technology in our lives. Given the destruction that Babel brings to the world, a hearty and resonant "No!" seems the right response. We theological types have our own mythologies. Every human community does. Ours includes the anti-Nazi theologians Karl Barth and Dietrich Bonhoeffer, who saw the anti-Jewish violence and the desecration of the Christian faith that was taking place in Germany and responded with a hearty "Nein!" Bonhoeffer responded with more, of course, paying for his opposition with his own life, joining the ranks of the martyrs. Barth often wished he had gone farther, joining Bonhoeffer and others in that white-robed army. The mythology works on us to have us say "Nein!" in as satisfying and Teutonic a way as possible. It is striking that this "Nein!" comes from across the theological spectrum, from liberal to conservative, Catholic to Pentecostal, orthodox to radical.

For example, Quentin Schultze wrote *Habits of the High-Tech Heart* some years ago now, before the internet had even taken over so much of our lives. Schultze, a professor of communication, writes that technology diverts "attention from the central concerns of life . . . to relatively trivial pursuits."[4] He could not be more right. Think here of a family gathered around a table paying no attention to each other, to God, or even to the food, but diverted instead to screens, tracking the most recent celebrity relationships or sports scores. Schultze rightly calls this a sort of "promiscuous knowing," a superficial attention that tends to the pornographic rather than to the sort of deep, committed knowledge of a marriage that bears fruit and builds households.[5] Schultze's title echoes that of an earlier landmark book, Robert Bellah's *Habits of the Heart*, which spoke of modernity's faith as whatever strikes our fancy, obeying only our own individual hearts. For Schultze, things seriously devolved between Bellah's apt description in 1985 to when Schultze published his book in 2002. Bellah cites an interviewee named Sheila who describes her DIY religion as Sheila-ism. That's modernity. Schultze speaks of an even more radical "selfism," cultivated by the "informationism" and "pseudo-intimacy" of the web. Modernity: dissolved. And to think, Schultze was writing before Facebook!

David Kelsey is one of Yale's great theologians, the sort of teacher who forever changes students' lives. He has written a multivolume and now-standard text on anthropology, the sort that will be consulted for years. He builds a positive foundation first, describing God as one who "delights in complex organic matter."[6] His visual image comes from the sports world—God pumping a fist and shouting "yes!" at the goodness of creation. The incarnation continues God's original delight in flesh: "What Jesus undergoes as a very complex organism decisively and normatively discloses who God is and how God is toward us."[7] As I often say in a preaching riff, God is not just almighty, all-knowing, all-present. God is those things, sure. But in Christ, God is also flesh: God has eyelashes and a spleen and a Jewish mom.

Over against this biblical portrait of a material-loving, flesh-becoming God, modern philosophy draws on ancient precedents and pulls body and spirit apart. Philosophers actually imagine whether we might be ghosts in a machine, spirits animating an improvable human shell. Computer scientists are hard at work making this actual: "There is no reason why my consciousness and intelligence could not be downloaded onto a computer that would then be me, or a replication of me."[8] The stuff of science fiction nightmares may soon be coming true in highly individualized super medicine, downloaded selves, technology as an escape from death. I am not exaggerating.

For both Schultze and Kelsey, this is simply the ancient heresy of Gnosticism, returned with a vengeance. Christians are often tempted to this heresy, and biblical passages can be contorted in its defense. It says that the body, the created world, even time and space, are distortions. Materiality is malicious. The goal of faith is to escape from this world, with its decay and death, into a realm without such monstrosities. Ancient Gnosticism appealed to those who thought of time and space, bodies and creation, as simply bound by decay and death. Surely this world is so bad it must have been made by mistake, caused by some titanic miscarriage. The world God intends will be perfect—and it is to that world that we must escape. Modern Gnosticism also regards this world as a sort of defective aberration. It is a machine that can be improved upon by technological genius. The body is a marvel but a flawed marvel, and its many flaws can be repaired with the right coding. And over against this, Schultze and Kelsey respond with a hearty, guttural "Nein!" "We are not spiritual souls contained in bodies, not ghosts in machines, not even centers of consciousness floating somehow above brains, but extraordinarily complex organic bodies."[9] God has this thing for creation. God made it under no external compulsion but only because God is always already community in the Triune life. Since God loves relationship, God made more relationships, with the spectacular array of creatures lovingly detailed in Genesis, lovingly redeemed by Christ, being made holy as God intends by the Holy Spirit. Creation is no error. It is God's delight.

The problem with this "Nein!" is that it overshoots. There is only one fall of humanity—the one recorded in Genesis, the effects of which are still very much with us. The mysterious serpent asks, "Did God say?" and we theologians have been repeating that question ever since, as Karl Barth points out. It is satisfying to fulminate against something being entirely wrong. But it is strange to do so on word processors, emailing manuscripts to publishers who then print and distribute books, promoting them on media old and new. Authors like these, like me (Jason), speak appreciatively of monasticism old and new as a response to technology. Yet monasteries use technology too—recruiting new religious, selling their products, curating monastic treasures for new generations. There is no escaping the world. In this world we are called to cultivate and take care of the land. That includes tool building, ingenuity, dexterity, all gifts from God. We do monstrously misuse those gifts. That's what this book is about: how to use them better.

Back in the innocent, carefree days of 2010, before quarantines and COVID-19, before Russian trolls and the reality-TV president, one of the most liberal seminaries in America hosted a conference called "Theology after Google." It drew liberal Protestants' most coveted badge of approval: attention from the secular press. The *Los Angeles Times* breathlessly announced that the Christian church "must embrace technology to survive."[10] One conference organizer toothily beamed, "We don't want you to silence your cell phones. We want you in this room to be connected to everything that's happening in the world." One academic praised the sort of "democratized religion" promised by the internet and compared it to the printing press, the glib analogy that birthed a google of equivocations. "Ladies and gentlemen," he grandly intoned, "we are talking today about a transition equally as great."[11]

This sort of eschatological language has long greeted the introduction of new technologies. One would expect the Christian church to be warier of false messiahs than that. These technologies are a marvel. They are also developed and run by the largest corporations in world history, generating wealth for a smaller and smaller portion of our populace, without much care to who might be using them to what nefarious purpose. Soon, Jeff Bezos will be a trillionaire and announce that his neighborhood in Seattle is seceding from the union to escape onerous taxation. I *think* I'm joking.

Secular cheerleaders can, perhaps, be forgiven for such mindless boosterism. Jeff Jarvis wrote one encomium, *What Would Google Do?*, about buying a Dell computer, complaining with a blog post that "Dell Sucks" when it would not work, and then finding that his post was #2 on Google in a search for Dell, coming up only after the company itself. Soon he was getting phone calls with promises of his money back. These companies have to be responsive. "Give the people control, and we will use it. Don't, and you will lose us."[12] Mark Zuckerberg of Facebook fame says his company is in the business of "elegant organization."[13] Facebook makes it easy, beautiful even, for friends to share life with one another, for communities to do what they do, maybe even "better" than IRL.

John Palfrey and Urs Gasser wrote *Born Digital* in 2008, and said that by 2000 there was more information posted online than had *ever* been published in books.[14] A lot more. Three million times more. Not a few writers have thought we might change the world through a blog or a podcast. Think again. In March 2019 there were 4.4 million blog posts published *every day*.[15] Good luck getting anyone's attention. *Born Digital* quotes a Harvard student comparing old media (books that reliably start and stop) to the web, where "there is no beginning and no end."[16] Online, folks can have as many fake selves as their time allows, creating avatar after avatar. Yet their "true" selves are set in cyberstone more than ever, with a history that is easy to trace, hard to forgive. The web is changing our very notion of the self, of human identity, of who we are and what we are *for*.

Do you hear all the theological echoes and resonances? Not just the cheesy book titles but also the more profound claim that we cannot simply talk from on high—instead we have to give away power, hear how people respond, and adapt. Church leaders know (or learn quickly) that people do not want to give their time, treasure, or attention to an institution merely to keep the institution running. They *are* willing, at times, to give their lives for something worthwhile. When the church makes it easier for them to do that, they'll turn their whole lives over to Christ through it. *Born Digital*'s theological echoes are only a little more oblique. The web aims for a sort of faux catholicity. It has unending knowledge; it is present everywhere; increasingly, it can even do the impossible for you. No wonder so many of us constantly gaze upon the glowing idols in our hands in a pose that looks not a little like worship.

On occasion Jason's suspicion of technology makes me jealous. I want to be the one who uses our digital tools with skepticism of their influence on me, with appropriate boundaries in place. Then again, I (Andria) also like to imagine myself living in an off-grid commune with chickens who don't have their own Instagram accounts. Ask anyone who knows me, however, and they'll tell you that if I ever have chickens, they'll have a handle. Ignoring our social technologies is not an option. Not because I grew up with trends like #CatSaturday and pics-or-it-didn't-happen but because I have seen Jesus alive and working in this place, redeeming lives on Facebook Messenger like it was the shore of the Gennesaret. I will not abandon this holy ground.

This inarguable work of the Spirit is a direct result of empowering people to serve and be served in this online space. But, as Jason argues, it is not an easy task. Part of moving our churches toward multifaceted ways of worshiping and being together is bringing our people along with us, and we don't tend to do this well. We have been telling the same story for two thousand years, and yet we struggle to live into its realized eschatology. The time ahead? The one Isaiah prophesied (Isa. 43:19)? It's here, and we're all part of it. Come!

Nothing made this paralysis more clear than when our aging mainline denominations made the desperate leap into cyberspace in response to our buildings being closed during the pandemic. The first question was, How do I find the internet? The second, What is YouTube? It was quickly apparent that the first job of the church was to equip the saints with the technological savvy that would enable them to remain part of the body.

A colleague of mine sent an email in those first few weeks of COVID-response stating she would have to conduct our meeting by chat box because she had lost her voice due to talking senior congregants through using Zoom. This wasn't in the job description, and nothing in seminary prepared her for it, but it was the only work worthwhile at the moment. How can we make the giving of one's life for the sake of the world easier, *online*?

We can start with the recognition that the longing to give and receive is one of the most essential spiritual needs we have. How many volunteer roles were forgotten or glossed over when worship ceased happening in the building? With a smaller percentage of people feeling fluent enough in technology to offer their time and talents, a significant number of people lost their only way of contributing to a community that had taught them that volunteering was the only way to be faithful. It is the beautifully disparate Babel, again.

Giving people an opportunity to build something beautiful is only as faithful as their understanding of *why* it is to be beautiful. If our people do not see the purpose in our online efforts and digital tools, their service will not be life-giving for them or for the church. But tell them the story of a time when all we had was papyrus and Roman roads, and they might rise with the bravery necessary for such a worthwhile mission.

An email entered my inbox one Monday several months into the process of individually walking congregants through a new video-conferencing platform. It came following an online discussion, and it read:

> Thank you all for an exciting evening. I closed my computer and found that my little grey cells were tingling with the joy and friendship and stimulation of our happy meeting. I realize that I arrived rather furtively but I am so pleased to have made my debut into Zoom World. I knew that you would be an accepting group for my fumbling approach and I was determined not to hinder your enjoyment of the meeting. Anyway, I felt I had been to a party.

We spend so much time trying to invite people into the place of action. *Build this! Clean this! Read this! Learn this!* But if we are to truly serve one another, perhaps the invitation requires a different address. Ah, to be the place of a party. Now that's Pentecost.

———————

The "answer," if there is one, to these bombastic claims that technology is damning or saving us is to offer less bombast. God alone is the one who saves (this is an underdetermined[17] response). The church is gathered by the Holy Spirit into the body of Christ in response to that saving work. Some of us who are being gathered tend to carry the entire internet around with us in our pockets. What do we do with these things? How can they be taken up into the work of the people of God in the world?

The "technology is damning us" people described above have good arguments. Christianity is an embodied faith. Gnosticism kills souls. The problem is they may slip unwittingly into another ancient heresy: that of Manicheism. We know we used this ancient Christian rival earlier; forgive us, we can only repeat ourselves. Manicheism posited that there are some things that are essentially good and other things that are essentially bad. These two are at war with each other, and the elect enlist on the side of the good and help it in various ways (details would divert us here). The orthodox said in response that no *thing* is essentially bad. Insofar as it is a thing, it is created by God, suspended by grace in existence rather than non-existence. You cannot go pick up a handful of evil. It has no actual substance. Evil is always parasitic on the good thing it is corrupting. Now of course these good thinkers are not Manicheans! But their arguments lean in that direction in their categorical and uniform denial of any goodness to be found in technology.

Here is a strange reality about the Christian church: it has always been a virtual body. Pentecost did not birth one congregation. It birthed a blizzard of congregations all over the known world (and to hear historians tell it—some of the peoples mentioned at Pentecost did not exist anymore or did not exist yet—this is not bad history; it is good theology). Ours is a going-and-telling faith, and not only on our physical feet. What does Paul do besides travel? He writes letters, some to churches that he never meets personally but where he still claims a sort of authority.[18] The church recognized this kind of virtual authority enough to keep those precious letters, pass them down, read them aloud across generations, and eventually canonize them as Scripture. In some cases Paul writes to churches he knows personally, churches he planted or pastored, and whose problems he knows well (the Corinthian correspondence, Galatians). In others he writes to churches he does not know personally, yet whom he clearly thinks will take his word seriously anyway (Romans). These letters were carried via road or boat, pondered, treasured, passed down and around, and eventually connected and called the "Word of God." In another portion of the New Testament, the writer tells his hearers that he would prefer to be with them in person. He cannot. So he has sent this letter instead, as a second-best option (2 John 12).[19] Face-to-face would be best, but failing that, here is this letter, a stand-in for a face, an image of an image. That second-best is part of the Bible! The New Testament is largely made up of such letters. A communal faith built on the incarnate and resurrected Christ requires bodily presence. But bodily presence is not always possible. So the church has always corresponded at a distance, and it *still conducted itself as church*—one body, bound together across space and time, worshiping one Lord. It is odd for Christianity, of all faiths, to say that it cannot do faith at a distance. It has been doing so since before it was even called "Christianity."

The practice of conducting ourselves Christianly continued into the early church. The Roman papacy did not appear all at once; instead, their church structure built up from the bottom over time—partly as a result of the exchange of letters. We love that something so ordinary and quotidian could build something so seemingly everlasting as church hierarchy! Rowan Williams describes the process this way: "By the third century (probably earlier), the simple custom of circular letters announcing the election of a new bishop and asking for prayers had become a standard feature of much Mediterranean church life. . . . To be excluded from this routine circulation of information and from the assurances of mutual prayers was . . . the main form of sanction and protest between churches."[20] Christianity *is* an epistolary faith, based on writings to and from friends who know one another in the flesh and others who do not yet—each equally part of the body of Christ. Some of the most thunderous debates in the history of theology came in letters between Saint Jerome and Saint Augustine, who never met but who circled each other in argumentation "like two scorpions," as a scholar friend of mine once said. They were in fleshly union enough to fight with one another like brothers. And the church kept their correspondence specifically to educate themselves and others in the depths of the faith. It is illuminating precisely as virtual correspondence between two very much flesh-and-blood (and warts!) human beings arguing at a distance.

I borrow this argument for the church as a virtual body from the great Oxford theologian Graham Ward.[21] Communications technology is changing the way we look at human beings, no doubt. We are less locally identifiable, less limited to any one place, more malleable, and even more international than we had thought. Ward has no objection to this, for the incarnation itself transgresses such boundaries. It is a modern fiction to think of a person as an individual, self-determining, a single soul in a single body in control of its destiny, "buffered" from all others, as Charles Taylor puts it.[22] Postmodern reaction to that view is closer to the mark in seeing human beings as interconnected, networked, changing in ways we're not always in control of—liquid rather than solid, if you will. Ward makes clear that some of the *nein*-sayers to digital church may be working out of nostalgia, pining for the good ol' days. But memory is a living thing, an active reception of God's creative and redeeming goodness, unfolding and never static. Postmodernity may be pushing us back behind modernity to an older memory of humanity, not as self-determining individuals but as a communal body, joined together in Adam as sinners and in Christ as those being saved. Decriers of technology worry that our very notion of humanity is under question. Ward helps us ask, What is "our" notion of humanity anyway? What if it owes more to Descartes than to Christ, and what if it *needs* unsettling?!

The question to ask about anything, technology included, is not whether it is entirely good or bad (an overly determined response). The question is how we can use it to love God and neighbor more. It can be used to augment relationship, to maintain contact over time and space. Augustine and Jerome used their day's technology to challenge one another so as to bless the whole church. But often they had to start by clarifying the chain of thought—did you get my letter from two years ago, or is that one at the bottom of the Mediterranean? I got your letter but it seems to respond to mine of three years back and not to my more recent one. Email is too fast, at times, leading us to fire off missives that gratify our self-righteousness while publicizing the half-baked and poorly digested. But it is an improvement on the fourth century's means of communication. Karl Barth and Eduard Thurneysen wrote letters to one another that illumine early twentieth-century Christian thought in central Europe. Sometimes they would bump into each other in their small town but refuse to talk: "I'm writing you a letter, let me finish first." The time we take in writing clarifies thought, regards the other, blesses the wider church and world. What scholar would not swim to the bottom of the Mediterranean for Paul's lost preliminary letter to the Corinthians or for a stack of lost Augustine/Jerome missives? We long for such communication because God speaks through letters, through relationships—even at a distance.

Note: long-distance correspondence is no substitute for face-to-face friendship, meals together, mutual prayer and worship and laughter and bodily touch, baptism and Eucharist. Digital communication is no substitute for, but rather a supplement to, embodied presence. It can extend, in weakened form, the goodness of community gathered around the eucharistic table and baptismal font. It cannot substitute for those things, even in extreme cases like prison or exile when it keeps us apart from one another for extended periods of time. It can, however, bear grace across time and space. We show this every time we open a Bible.

We can do more than exchange letters with one another at a distance. We can also teach online. I respect institutions that have refused to do this. Out of a commitment to embodied life and sacramental theology, they view distance teaching as a defective product that must be resisted. Or, as one teacher says to me, "I do distance education. It's called 'writing books.'" This view changed quickly with the COVID-19 crisis in 2020, though it was inadequate before that. Think with me of a seminary student working multiple jobs, taking care of multiple family members, flying into class at the last second, missing the first few minutes, trying hard to stay awake, and not having done the reading. That is technically an in-person student, doing it poorly. Think now of a distance student, preparing hard, ready on time, and on the edge of her seat. She has not moved from her home or community or the church that raised her, equipped her, started her in ministry, and encouraged her to study further. On the contrary, she is applying what she is studying to that ministry, and she is growing in effectiveness and confidence. It is, of course, important not to compare the best version of one thing with the worst iteration of another. I just wonder if the second student might be more embodied than the first, wherever their bodies presently are.

One might suspect some traditionalist theological voices to be nervous about extending the church's ministry online. Robert Jenson, for example, was a student of Karl Barth's and a curmudgeon of sorts who always had the *nein!* button near his trigger finger. Yet he did not say a simple no to online theological education. Technical things can be taught online, such as languages or simple history. The sacrament should not be celebrated online, he thought. Just as there are things that can only be experienced on the computer in diminished, voyeuristic fashion, like eating or sex or friendship, so there are things that should only be done face-to-face, like breaking the loaf, pouring the water. Yet theology itself can be conducted online. It is not a first-order discourse, like prayer or celebration of the sacraments. It is a second-order discourse, reflecting on the language of the people of God. It's worth noting that Jenson *was* a theologian, blessing the church with two volumes of systematic theology and hundreds of other challenging articles. His very life's work could go online with little problem.[23] I once asked Stanley Hauerwas why we saw so few new initiatives in institution-building among Protestants. We once traversed the continent liberally throwing up colleges and hospitals, universities and seminaries, camps and high schools in our wake. He agreed, in one way an era of institution-building may be over. But in another way, he challenged the premise. How do we know that we're not building important new institutions at present? Then he said it: many of these new technological endeavors could prove to be very important in time.[24] This from a man who didn't used to check his own email, who answers the phone on the first ring. He is stuck in the 1970s technologically. Yet he grants the Holy Spirit may have work to do online.

I notice some of the most effective pastors use digital communication to "increase their pastoral touches."[25] There are things parishioners will not go to their pastor with but for some reason will disburden about on social media. It's easy to find out—just friend them. Then pray for them. That's your job. Using emails and blogs and podcasts and other media old and new can do the same work. Or to switch the metaphor, it can be like Jesus's farmer, slinging seed everywhere. Some gets in folks' hair and some goes in the road and some gets eaten by animals, but some takes root and grows. Don't carefully farm, only putting seed in studiously delineated rows. Throw it everywhere, wantonly, indiscriminately, and even digitally. Even climate change apocalypticists agree. Bill McKibben, working hard to help the church take climate change seriously, insists we will all be driving less in the future.[26] So we will need the internet in order not to be too parochial, to remain engaged with the world.

Most of us won't be able to avoid using technology. It is just too useful a way to network, communicate, preach, and teach. Its ease is also its curse, of course. That very ease allows us to be our worst selves in public, allows Russian trolls to influence US elections, and opens us all up to surveillance and cybercrime. Those are the parasitic evils on a good thing. We must use it while also drawing attention to how it malforms us and others, how it inhibits love of God and neighbor. Because it does. All created things do in this age before Christ's return. We need some radical persons and communities saying no to things to remind us of their harmful nature. But most of us will say a qualified yes. Qualified how?

One victim of digital technology is the physical newspaper. This staple of modern culture has proven unprofitable without classified ads (cannibalized by free online services), and so it continues to teeter on the edge of existence. Hegel once pointed out that ancient people got up in the morning and said their prayers; modern people get up in the morning and read their newspapers. There was something nearly devotional about it. The newspaper was not inherently good—it was always a competitor for our attention (even if it wasn't as effective a competitor as Twitter now is). But one casualty that goes with it is the city itself. Richard Rodriguez asks if we can have a modern city without a newspaper. What holds all the buildings in the Bay Area together as much as the *San Francisco Chronicle*, attuning people to a common set of stories and worries? His words:

> The other day I came upon a coffeehouse that resembled, as I judged from its nineteenth-century exterior, the sort of café where the de Young brothers might have distributed their paper. The café was only a couple of blocks from the lively gay ambience of upper Market Street yet far removed from the clamorous San Francisco of the nineteenth century. Several men and women sat alone at separate tables. No one spoke. The café advertised free wi-fi; all but one of the customers had laptops open before them. . . . The only sounds were the hissing of an espresso machine and the clattering of a few saucers. A man in his forties, sitting by the door, stared at a screen upon which a cartoon animal, perhaps a dog, loped silently.[27]

The scene is more morgue than café. The place Rodriguez describes may as well be in Cairo or Singapore as in the Bay Area—it is a scene of anonymous people in a no-place. This is a sort of faux-catholicity. I say "faux" because it is false to squash the local and particular in favor of the universal. By contrast, genuine catholicity honors the local and particular while gathering it up into a larger universal.

Notice how many saints have their place names after their Christian ones (Augustine of Hippo; Teresa of Kolkata). The whole church is present in any local gathering, and the local origins of saints, ideas, and devotions are not obliterated as they are passed on to bless the rest of the church. Universals that purport to drop from the sky and squash the local are out of balance, catholically speaking. Right now in every remote village in Africa or Asia, a young woman is working her hardest to understand a local language's idiosyncrasies so she can translate the Bible into her friends' heart-tongue. The same village has a pin on the map in that provincial or national capital, pushed there by an executive who wants to teach everyone English so as to sell them hamburgers. While many moderns have been suspicious of missions and uncritical about fast food or capitalism, catholic thought and practice would honor the local, the intimate, the granular, while also blessing the world. Capitalism has no similar claim to cherish the local or particular for their own sake.

One criterion, then, for faithful use of the web is how it can help us be *more* local, more particular, more granular in our attention to the specific patch of ground to which God has called us to do ministry. And here the internet can do wonders. The church in any one place can describe how it is witnessing to Jesus Christ in its local particularity in order to help the church in another place witness to the resurrection in its. Neither is eclipsed, left behind, bypassed, or flattened in some larger whole. Each is the entire church, all the church there is, as it honors its place and others'. No doubt the web has Gnostic, body-denying tendencies. So too does the Christian church (Gnostics had their favorite verses too). Yet God can make a promise from soil that looks simply unpromising to our eye (indeed—it may not even be soil! It may be the sidewalk!). The church, like Christ's sower, is always tossing seed everywhere, not carefully calibrating where would be a waste, what destination is no good for our seed, not meticulously holding back for more promising opportunities. No, we fling it every place.[28] Some of it will land even here, online. And when that happens, our stance cannot be that of the scold, telling God or others that nothing good can happen in such digital places as Nazareth. It has to be the response of faithfulness that should always be coming from our mouths: none other than "hallelujah."

- Can you think of a case in which faithfulness has sprung up almost accidentally, despite human action? Extra credit for an instance of this online!

- A prayer after the presentation of the elements in Catholic Mass asks for God's blessing on both the bread and the wine, made from the elements of the earth as they are but then also *remade* as "the work of human hands." If our human making can be offered to God before God offers it back to save us, can specifically digital work be so offered? If so, how?

FOUR

Jesus's Own Family

And [Jesus] replied, "Who are my mother and my brothers? . . . Whoever does the will of God is my brother and sister and mother."

Mark 3:33–35

This is Jesus's not-altogether-polite response to an entreaty to meet with his biological family. Mary and the boys had come to see Jesus out of concern: he seems to be beside himself. They mean to restrain him. As far as we can tell, he won't meet with them. Family? What family? Whoever does the will of God is my family. You can read it all for yourself, right there in Mark 3:31–35. According to the rest of the New Testament and the church's tradition, Mary and James and the others came around. We call Mary the "mother of God" for a reason; and James became the leader of the Jerusalem church for a reason. Jesus's biological family started on the outs with him, but they came around to faith. Sometimes it takes the best of us a while to get on the right track with God in our immediate family.

One of the common charges levied against the digital revolution is what it does to the family. I (Jason) am hesitant to preach that particular jeremiad since, to read the Gospels, Jesus of Nazareth is actually the biggest threat there is to the nuclear family. This chapter will argue that families can indeed flourish despite threats both digital and christological. Yet we do need some people to say no to the screens, the way the church has always had a few people say no to such goods as money, sex, and power. What might that "no" look like, and how does it inform those of us who say a halting "yes" instead?

This is not the only hint of trouble in Jesus's immediate family. He is, you may have heard, born without any human father. Joseph, Mary's betrothed, takes this about as well as any cuckold could: he intends to dismiss Mary quietly, without disgrace (Matt. 1:19). But an angel reassures him the child is really God's. Sure, every surprisingly pregnant unmarried teenager in history might claim that the child is from God, but this one really is. Joseph goes ahead with the marriage. But the church's iconographic tradition often portrays Joseph in Jesus's Nativity off in the corner, sulking. Sometimes he is being counseled by a cloven-hoofed figure. Old scratch is, presumably, whispering the rumors in Joseph's ear that the child is not God's at all but the son of some other man. Iconographers weigh in on this gossip by making Joseph appear so old and frail that he cannot possibly have fathered the child himself. Tucked into the wild story of Jesus's first sermon in his hometown is what could be a slanderous reference to his questionable patrimony. "Is not this Joseph's son?" his hearers ask (Luke 4:22). Pretty soon, Jesus is picking a fight with the townies, and they escort him to the edge of a cliff (4:29).

It is surprising that some recent political movements have claimed Jesus's sanction for their championing of "family values." Jesus himself would have been called names equivalent to our word "bastard." His family of origin seems to have rejected him, at least for a time. He responds by rejecting them back—and the whole town along with them. Some of Jesus's most avid early followers had no biological family of their own. Taking their cues from Jesus's celibacy and Paul's teaching (1 Cor. 7), early Christians often did not marry. Christ is coming soon—so why spend time and energy on any other spouse? This was a remarkable abdication of their Jewish responsibility to fill the earth and multiply, and it made them look ridiculous in the eyes of their pagan neighbors. Who gives up sex for . . . Jesus? Those who believe in another sort of family—they called one another "sister" and "brother." And those who believe in another sort of power—Christ will renew the church by conversion if necessary, not only by biological propagation.[1]

This is the first Christian thing to say about the family: no one has to make a new one. We *do* apparently have to come from one—since Adam and Eve, at least, we all tend to have belly buttons. But we do not have to marry or have children to be whole persons in Christ. Baptism initiates us into the only family that matters—the one called "church." And in this family those whose family of origin is broken will find plenty of company, starting with Jesus. In this family we are all adopted daughters and sons, elevated to be siblings of our big brother Jesus by the Holy Spirit of God (Rom. 8:14–17). Jesus disrupts biological families and makes a new one.

For not a few of us, our biological families have been disrupted not so much by Jesus as by technology. How many times do you see a family sitting together at a table, faces glued to glowing blue rectangles, nearby people made far away and faraway people seeming more near? How many times have you *been* those people, "alone together"? The table is the place where Jesus saves us with bread and wine, where every meal points forward to another meal at the end of all things, with Christ as host, the poor as guests of honor, and maybe even the rest of us snuck in through the servants' door. When we dine right in the meantime, it is a foretaste of this eschatological banquet. When we don't . . . hold on a sec, I gotta take this call . . .

In one way, we shouldn't be too judgmental about technology disrupting families. The very best futurists(!), engineers, and advertising people on the planet have spent oceans of money to addict all of us to the little devices. In another way, judge we must. Just think of an elderly mom and her digital-native daughter or granddaughter sitting together, one ignored, the other texting away. Or of the couples broken apart because one or both settled for online intimacy in place of embodied intimacy. Or of the children who know more about celebrities than the parents or siblings just beside them in body, lightyears away in attention. Technology can tie people together, no doubt: grandparents or deployed soldiers or students off at school or folks separated by quarantine can commune face-to-face in ways that we could not have imagined in previous centuries. It can also undo a family even more quickly than faith in Jesus could in biblical times.

We should define some terms, of course. Technology is different from the mere use of tools. Andy Crouch's fantastic book *The Tech-Wise Family* makes this abundantly clear.[2] Humans have used tools since, well, we've been human. We don't have sharp fangs or long claws or tough exteriors to defend ourselves—we have big brains. So we use tools. *Homo faber*, we've called ourselves: the person who makes stuff. But tools used to stay in their place. A pick stays in the field; a weapon is for the hunt or battlefield; a vehicle stays near the road. The little gods in our pockets will not stay in their place.

Technology claims an omnipresence once reserved for God alone. Its great promise is to make everything easy. Biblical people once thought of the Sabbath as God's way of rest, but every technological advance promises more leisure time to be with family or relax on one's own. That moment of eschatological bliss never seems to arrive. Tools are still handy. They take skill and persistence and a community of wise users to employ them well. Technology requires no skill. You just turn on the machine and you can have whatever you want, whenever you want it. Crouch contrasts a tool, like a guitar, with technology, like a guitar app.[3] Skilled guitar players learn their trade with painstaking practice over countless hours. They earn those callouses on their fingers. They learn best in a community that sprawls across centuries, made up of people both living and dead. Guitar App pretends to provide skill but does not, cannot, produce it. Jonathan Wilson-Hartgrove, author and activist, says of his children's use of technology that he knows he can't take their phones away. But he can insist they learn an instrument as well.

Philosopher Albert Borgmann, Crouch's mentor on matters technological, contrasts what he calls a "focal practice" with technology's "device paradigm."[4] A focal practice is a complex activity whose goods are internal to the practice. You don't learn guitar to have more dexterous fingers, though that may be a side effect. You learn guitar to . . . learn guitar. You play and others listen, join in, even sing. Ours may be the first generations in human history only to listen to music professionally produced by others and seldom to play it. That's what "professionals" do, technologically enhanced, for money. In ages past, folks played music together however skilled or not. It was participatory, not professional, and it was not produced by devices.

Borgmann's key example is the way we heat our homes. Ancient peoples and many today heat their homes with fire. A hearth is then the center of the house. You put the household gods by the hearth. The fire is the place where stories are told, where younger generations discover who they are. They learn things, like how not to get burned! More importantly, they learn stories that frame who they are and that explain what sort of world this is. They also learn more mundane, but not less important, things: how to gather the right firewood and how to maintain that fire. Cooking happens over the hearth. Younger children were cared for by older generations who maintained an honored place in the family.

Crouch is fascinated by the way our eyes dart across glowing blue rectangles now the way human eyes used to dart at the fingers of flame warming us, our food, our generations.[5] Things have not improved. Borgmann contrasts the hearth with central heating.[6] It requires no skill from users at all—just an expertly skilled repairman, one who occasionally comes at great expense. It hides its own means of production behind walls and in basements. The massive energy required is skillfully hidden from most of us most of the time. It gathers no people. It hosts no stories, passes on no skill, invites no worship. It just works, if the bill is paid, with no depth of wisdom or grace extended. Crouch encourages families to eat by candlelight, sit by firelight, tell stories and sing—why wait for a blackout?[7] Our ancestors had little choice. We do. And we hardly ever take it.

Borgmann shows why. He writes of two brothers "famished for something to read" in the Bitterroot Valley of Montana in 1860.[8] They heard of a trunk of books—150 miles away. They crossed three dangerous rivers to get to them, and they spent half their money on five of the books. They say, "But then we had the blessed books, which we packed carefully in our blankets, and joyfully started on our return ride of a hundred and fifty miles. Many were the happy hours we spent reading those books."[9] Would that we treasured reading so much again—it's no accident that our not having to work so hard to procure reading material goes hand in hand with not caring about it.

The first people to see Yellowstone raised a shout of praise to their Creator, no doubt. A rabbi friend of mine talks about watching tourists approach the Grand Canyon and listening to what they say. Most curse—something related to the bedroom or the bathroom. Some say things like "Holy cow!" which is sort of religious, but it refers to somebody *else's* religion. My friend and his family say the Jewish blessing in the presence of natural wonders: "Blessed art thou, O Lord God, King of the universe, for thou has done great things on earth and in heaven." How much better is that than approaching a natural wonder with an eye to the best selfie to post to social media? Is it any wonder that every year folks *die* trying to get a better shot? Those who approach Yellowstone or the Grand Canyon have seen it from a thousand vantages in film or online. We compare "reality" with these preconceptions (as one Hollywood jokester marveled at seeing a natural wonder: "It's like a screensaver!"[10]). We fiddle with our camera phones, unmoved, and then walk away, leaving the Creator unpraised. Two brothers in the Bitterroot Valley in 1860 risked their lives and spent half their fortune on five books to pass the winter; on our phones we can read nearly anything that's ever been written, and we hardly care at all.

It is easy to wax nostalgic when critiquing technology. It has made good on so many of its promises. It has delivered humanity from the terrifying reign of diseases that once wiped out millions (and today we look to it for a new cure). Chance a walk around a cemetery with graves older than seventy-five years and notice how many tiny headstones you see and how many husbands with multiple markers for wives who died on or around the same day as one of those poor infants. Indigenous people and African Americans are often rightly skeptical of white people claiming previous centuries were better. Indentured Indigenous peoples and kidnapped Africans *were* the technologies that made life easier for the European colonizers. Even granting the power of Borgmann's hearth example above, who really wants to go back on central heating?! Even if one wanted to, there is no putting the genie back in the bottle. Just try telling your in-laws you plan to go without electricity and see how fast the authorities make it to your door to take your kids away.

Technology is never an unadulterated good. It is, in fact, a Christian heresy to say so. Technology claims to deliver the kingdom without the king: a life of ease and grace, free from crushing labor (for those on the "have" side of the ledger anyway). Rumsfeld or Cheney or some other of W's warlords once justified America's military adventurism with a nighttime glance at the Korean peninsula. Democratic and prosperous South Korea was fully lit up at night. Communist and authoritarian North Korea was nearly entirely dark, with only a few pinpricks around Pyongyang. American lives lost: worth it. You can't fight the eschaton.

Christians, of all people, should be able to spot a false theology when we see one. Technology is not the savior, and the technological age is not the messianic one. We should be able to spot this because we helped create it. For example, a researcher in quantum computing and artificial intelligence told a gathering of Christian seminarians they should let go of any hope of a spiritual heaven. For he had something even better: soon we will be able to transfer human identity to the cloud. At death, we can be uploaded into a computer, where we can, presumably, never die again.[11] He may be right, such transhumanist "salvation" may be nigh. But isn't it interesting that he feels the need to compete with Christian notions of heaven? What other language will he borrow to herald his coming accomplishment? This is just the latest entry in a long legacy of trumpeting technological "progress" with Christianese. The church, of all people, should have eyes to see it and the courage to denounce it.

One way to do that is with a little history. We rarely remember false steps on the road to progress. Spiritualism was a Christianish sort of faith that took its bearings from the telegraph. If Mr. Morse's invention could help you communicate with people unseen halfway around the globe, spiritualism's séances could help you communicate with people unseen on the other side of the veil of death. Its technology included Ouija boards and trances, and those grieving after the Civil War and World War I swore by its successes.[12] The line between technology and magic can be hard to discern at times.[13] Another example: Ruha Benjamin of Princeton shows that hiring- and health-care software promises to remove racial bias from the health care field. But *who* programs the software? Our unwitting bias is often written into such programs, which then produce purportedly neutral data that says who not to hire or who doesn't get life-saving treatment. There are no non-sinners available, unfortunately. The promised source of salvation blinds us to our whitewashed sins.[14]

The West has been the source of much technological innovation for the last half millennium, and the West has been nominally Christian for some of that time—it is no surprise that technology comes gift wrapped in Christian presumptions and boosterism. Elsewhere in this book we will say more about the good and gospel-filled things that technology makes possible. We see why folks would be tempted to make an eschatology out of technology—it has made our lives easier, longer, and, in some instances, better. But this chapter about the family is more about technology's false hopes, and the need to resist. How do those called to make their lives with others in a family resist the allure of devices and love one another, face-to-face, on the way to loving God together?

———————

I have often told ministry colleagues not to refer to the church as a family. They mean it to be a warm, inclusive description. I actually find it off-putting, and I'm not alone. Mine is the first generation where you can ask a perfect stranger *when* their parents got divorced. A step-half-removed relation of some sort asked my brother at a wedding one time, "Hey, aren't you my brother?" (Answer: no, I'm not, unless we're talking theology . . .) Between divorce and remarriage and test tubes and surrogates and steps and halves and quarters, it's hard to tell who is related to whom. And, finally, who cares? A family is not made by DNA. A family is made by difficult promises made and kept, not necessarily to those who share genetic data but to those who share space under a roof, to those who share a story, pray together, a table, a bed, a life. Gay and lesbian Christians who've been disowned by their disapproving families first taught me about *chosen* families—the people you bind yourself to and vice versa, family by grace rather than nature. As Robert Frost has written, "Home is where, when you have to go there, they have to take you in."[15] Now the norm, bordering on cliché, is that family is the people who harm you. No wonder the movie theaters and liquor stores make such a killing during the holidays (that last word a misnomer from its origins if there ever was one). Family: people who spend holidays using the same Wi-Fi signal.

But then something odd happens. You find yourself in a family. And you're determined to do it "better" than it was done to you. You've made difficult and beautiful promises to a spouse. Children and grandparents and assorted others have come into the family via birth or adoption or hospitality-turned-family. Any group of people living together has to abide by rules if food is to be cooked, homes cleaned, people transported, school attended, worship to God offered. Technology affects all those activities and thus our commitments. The determination to do family "right" can be its own sort of graceless arrogance, as if "we" are not susceptible to the same pressures and failures and vicissitudes as those under which our parents suffered. Our life is made by mercy, not moral sternness. All the same—how do we do it as best we can? And how do we have the devices bring life to our costly commitments rather than death?

We're not sure. We just know it's hard. Crouch has some outstanding suggestions, including three choices: choose character, shape space, and structure time.[16] Character: family exists to move one another toward wisdom and courage. Screens can't do that. Only God's Spirit, working through Christian community, can. Shape space: move technological devices, like the television, to places where they do not dominate family space. Put them somewhere uncomfortable (my son recently complained that the television was at an awkward angle for long-term viewing: progress!). And structure time: let there be Sabbath time set aside that is free from devices, not only one day a week but also hours each day, a day a month, and a week a year (even more boldly—in the Bible the Israelites, in an agricultural economy, were to leave land fallow for one *year* in seven!). Crouch also suggests specific Christian disciplines like solitude, fasting, and silence.[17] Like anyone trying to improve at anything, this takes practice, mutual encouragement, grace, and seriousness. And he also has brilliant specific examples: put the phones to bed before you go to bed. Spend the waking hours in prayer, not on screens. Pastor Aaron Miller, our friend here in Vancouver, has always preached that liturgy needs to live at home. Christians must relearn this from our Jewish forebears—the table and hearth are where we practice faith. During COVID-19, Miller's church finally started to believe him. And you know what? Two or three times the number of people are also showing up for worship online. He thinks there's no going back. Apparently, we can be, to use a new cliché, both high-tech and high-touch. Sacramentally bound in family and also worshiping on the screen.

The Christian church has resources at hand with which to counter the places that devices have colonized our lives. We just don't notice them.

Perhaps, as one church leader suggests, we're only now coming to realize the detriments that devices are in our family life and only now recognizing that we need to do something about it. Cherie White is a former leader with the Salvation Army, which you'll notice is disproportionately represented in places of financial and spiritual deprivation. If you want to find innovative work among the poor, find the Salvation Army. Cherie left her job with them largely because it had become middle class. She and her husband, Aaron, live on the Downtown Eastside of Vancouver with some of the poorest, most addicted people in all of Canada. The Whites relocated to be near Jesus's dearest friends. Aaron tells the story of a woman shrieking in the alley the first night they lived there. Moment of truth: Do you tell the children what's really happening? He did: "Baby, that woman is in pain. She's in so much pain she took a bit of poison to feel better, but now she's out of poison and feels worse." The Whites' daughter responded with a question that has moved them since, and, frankly, haunts my dreams: "What's her name?"[18]

The Whites are convinced that community is the answer to poverty. Jesus gathers us into a new people, over against the fractured, lonely selves who turn to substances to numb pain. So the Whites invite friends and strangers into their home. Folks in detox sleep on their couch. They will not leave people to rot in alleys. Instead, like the man in Jesus's parable of the Good Samaritan, they bring them home to get well. And for this, they've found themselves called on the carpet, marched into boardrooms by denominational bureaucrats. Don't they know they're risking a lawsuit? What about safety? There are kids in the house! The lawyers are not wrong, in one sense. But the Whites are busy being Christian. And they are no mere nuclear family. The folks coming into their home become *part* of their family. Their children are disciplined in three languages (Spanish when things get *really* bad, Cherie said). A French-Canadian in recovery helps their children with French homework. Their children are growing up as Christians: people who make room in our lives the same way God has made room for us in Christ. And the lawyers can't do a thing to stop it.

Cherie White's new work is as an entrepreneur. When Vancouver's housing market was still scalding hot, she bought buildings and flipped them. This caused some marital strife. Aaron thought she was lending to the grotesque inequality problem we have in housing in Vancouver. Cherie's answer was that she was wringing capital from the market to house vulnerable friends. She'd seen a cycle where friends would get sober, live in missional community for a year, and then be turned out and wind up back in the alley, newly addicted. She couldn't let that happen, so she turned a commercial profit to house the vulnerable. The market cooled, so she's recently hired a handful of friends in recovery to do renovations for her, mostly cosmetic stuff. Her project manager, Charlie, once fell six stories when a cable failed while working on another company's site. Charlie had just bought kneepads *that day*, in response to a nudge from God. They may have saved her life. Her wrists were shattered and now are mechanically repaired—a gift from our technological age—but they leave her feeling "crippled."

"Why would you hire a cripple like me?" Charlie asks Cherie often.

"Charlie!" Cherie responds, "Because you defied death!"

Charlie is also a woman in the trades (rather unique, that), leading other tradespeople in doing excellent work—work that takes painstaking practice and years of training and that cannot be done via an app. And this is not just business. White's office for Kingdom Realty is in the Downtown Eastside, at Jackson and Hastings, with a commitment to welcoming whoever walks in, for whatever reason: "We drop everything." Cherie pines for a moment, "I could be downtown with a view of the harbor. . . ."

And Cherie avoids lots of technology. Not all of it—she texts often and returns calls—but she grows her business face-to-face (not via

email—"I get one response in one hundred to emails; face-to-face I
get ten out of ten"). I asked Cherie to speak about social entrepre-
neurship to a class, and students were duly impressed. They asked
the obvious question: How do you accomplish so much? Simple, she
said. You know how you spend all day on social media, all night on
Netflix? Stop it. Now. "People tell me they binge-watch, they scroll
all day. I don't. Who has the time?" This may have been the first time
that members of Gen Z heard that their screens are evil. Look at all
they can accomplish simply by switching the devices off! But then the
Salvation Army does have a certain starch in its shirts. Cherie tells
of Charlie's conversion in prison. After Charlie had contemplated
suicide, an older woman from the Army came and visited with her.
"It's Jesus or hell, dear." She took the road less traveled.

It's not that Cherie White has figured everything out. She just
knows that some of her worst instincts are exacerbated by the devices.
She, too, binge-watches or scrolls when she's tired, when she wants
to avoid people, and when she's checked out of community. That's
why she makes those things difficult for herself to do. "We're looking
to buy farmland for an intentional community—we *might* get Wi-Fi
out there!" The Whites watch Netflix—together, once a week, tuning
into *Lost*. They don't buy phones or data plans for their kids. "We
see it as our duty to provide housing, education, clothes, food. Not
phones. Get a job." The kids do, and still their phones are monitored
and subject to confiscation.

Cherie goes to Catholic Mass now a few times a week and sits in
silence. That's the hardest thing for her, but it's perfectly anti-social:
"People don't even look at you when they pass the peace!" she gushes.
Then she prays with the homeless in a tent city. "I'm not going to
church so much anymore, I am the church," she says, tentatively, as if
she's doing it wrong somehow, and as if she is not in church worshiping several times per week. *Being* the church with more vulnerable
friends yields some surprising insights. Her poorer friends on the
Downtown Eastside don't lack access to the web. They're online a
lot—sometimes for nefarious purposes, usually not sitting and scrolling social media but often buying and selling. Whatever digital divide
exists out there, it isn't the one we'd imagined: lack of access. Nor is
poverty a matter of lack of cash. "Folks handle thousands of dollars

a day," Cherie said. Poverty is a mindset, a fractured set of relationships, not a lack of capital. "When a little girl is sexually abused at age five, she learns a lesson: she is only good for sex. The unlearning of that lesson can only happen in community, where she learns how treasured she is."

Cherie may fear she's doing "church" wrong, but let me reassure, she is not. I've seen how she does church. When I was doing an interim pastoral gig in Vancouver at a tall-steeple, country-club church, Cherie came one time. But she didn't come alone. She brought Jesus with her. He was in disguise as an older woman in a wheelchair, still a patient at the hospital nearby, clearly in physical distress but also in spiritual joy. The two worshiped like free people, hands up, with regular shouts and amens, drawing stares. It was as if Cherie was worried we wouldn't have Jesus at church, so she brought him along. "We thought we were going to lose her," she said of her friend. But her friend refused to die. She's a survivor of residential schools here in Canada—the effort by churches to separate Indigenous people from their culture and to Europeanize them, an effort that only ended in the mid-1990s. "I'm not dying," her friend said. "I need to fight for residential school survivors!"[19]

Cherie's friend's name is Grace.

Grace comes in many forms—some farther from the church. God seems to have left gifts everywhere, indiscriminately—the way Jesus farms. And some of those are among beloved but not religious people. Sven Birkerts is one. I still remember the look he gave me when I told him what a theologian is (that is, someone who studies God). He's an essayist, memoirist, editor, and writing instructor. And he is a critic of technology. For a non-religious person, he sure reaches for religious language to denounce it. To wit: "The gathered weight of literary expression, what we used to consider our cultural ballast, is fading."[20] We're losing the ability to concentrate for long stretches, to follow a story line. Our habits of attention are under great duress from new habits like grazing and scrolling. His evidence is, of course, anecdotal, based on observing himself and his spouse and his kids and his students, but his experience resonates.

The kind of reading necessary to tackle great books and works of art may be receding.

The skills to write such works are atrophying as well. Birkerts doesn't just mean that publishing is under duress and fewer works of fiction are coming out, though that's true.[21] Birkerts means that humanity itself is under revision. "What is imagination if not the animating power of inwardness?"[22] Birkerts asks. The steeping of a private self in deep time allows souls to flourish. He looks at his own kids and asks if they will ever know the slow drip, drip, drip of time. He notices that silence is now exceptional. And the imagination that once "burrowed its way into idleness" (a great phrase) is now superseded by the glowing screen, the clicking thumbs. In order to live a life of reading and writing (and, we might add, prayer), one needs a sense of friction, of mystery, of gravity, of contradiction—all things that require time and a self and no distractions, at the least. What's happened instead is that since the middle of the last century we have introduced device after device to interrupt that idleness. And Birkerts is not happy about it. He wants none of the balance that will see something good in all things. He calls himself "an unregenerate reader." As we quoted earlier, he originally concluded his book with a jeremiad that would make a street preacher blush:

> The devil no longer moves about on cloven hooves, reeking of brimstone. He is an affable, efficient fellow. He claims to help us all along to a brighter, easier future, and his sales pitch is very smooth. . . . Fingers tap keys, oceans of fact and sensation get downloaded, are dissolved through the nervous system. Bottomless wells of data are accessed and manipulated, everything flowing at circuit speed. Gone the rock in the field, the broken hoe, the grueling distances. . . . From deep in the heart I hear the voice that says, "Refuse it."

So what happened to soften that critique? Birkerts had kids. And they multitask. And they pile device upon device. And he couldn't just refuse it. He and his wife chose instead "artful seduction"; they surround their children with books and try to lure them into the good life of loving to read. He also wanted to continue writing, and that's hard to do without email (though Wendell Berry pulls it off).

He calls himself a more divided critic now, but he still likes his earlier bombastic self. So do I. When I interviewed him for *Faith & Leadership*, I found him not only convincing but also without a cell phone (somehow we still located each other at the airport). He had ideas for a Sabbath from digital technology—like European citizens whose countries offer generous maternity leave, he thought we should have creativity leave, where we can open back up the long distance in the soul that makes creativity possible.[23]

Birkerts reminds us to mourn the web. It's a created good, the work of our hands, and an astonishing one at that. But like all human works, it's fallen. We might say it gives us more of everything that's human: more of the glory (all the church fathers are available online now in all sorts of translations) and all of the shame (someone told me years ago that I just *had* to use Reddit—a social media site that provides people a place to post articles, videos, and memes from around the web and lets viewers vote on their favorites. The story with the most votes that day was about University of Michigan pranksters who posted a fake sign about a new anti-masturbation policy in showers. Thanks for sharing[24]). It can make previously impossible things possible, indeed. Missionaries traveling across continents once had to wait years to receive a letter, then years more for a reply to reach home. Now we can reach almost anyone on the planet at once, and we all yawn. Sure, communication is easier, more reliable now. But the deeper point is that we are failing to develop the sort of depth of soul required to have a conversation worth having.

Let me tell you about another family trying to make its way in the world awash with technology. Baker and Patience Perry were once undergraduates and athletes at Duke University. Patience was a field hockey player who suffered a broken arm in a game. Instead of slinking to the sidelines or waiting to be helped off the field, she picked herself up and attacked the opposing player who'd injured her. She impressed a man named Eustace Conway, a legendary naturalist, subject of a book by Elizabeth Gilbert called *The Last American Man*, and later, even more strangely, a reality-TV star.[25] Gilbert's book chronicles Conway doing things like picking up roadkill on the way to class at a local university and then demonstrating how to safely eat it *in front of the class*.[26] Dude's not into technology.

He lives in the woods, the way he thinks we all should. People join him and learn outdoor skills. When asked about what technology he misses, Conway says he'd love him some plastic buckets. They can make wicker containers, but they're far from waterproof. Not what I'd have picked, but never mind. Another kid who was on a field trip asked Conway whether he could survive if he were plopped down naked in the Arctic. "Probably," Conway said. "But it'd really help if I had a knife." A knife is another handy piece of technology, alongside clothes, tools to start a fire, and food. Patience joined Conway as his love interest, and she provides the moral ballast. She leaves the relationship, and the book, when Conway builds an open-air, lightweight buggy in which to circumnavigate the Great Plains. That part sounds fun. Only, he proceeds to drive the team and themselves so hard that they don't have fun. Turns out he didn't just mean to circle the plains. He meant to claim the overland wagon all-time speed record for that ride. Patience didn't sign up for that, and she drops out of the story.

She later dropped into Baker's life.

Baker was his own extraordinary combination of athlete and nerd. He attended Duke while Coach Krzyzewski's crew was on a rare downswing. Injuries piled up, and Coach K asked his players who on campus was good enough to play in the ACC—the premier college basketball league in the US. They mentioned Baker. So Coach K (as we call him) called the office of the dean of students and asked for Baker. "Oh boy," the dean said. Baker was off the grid, living in a shack in Duke Forest. He attended class, played pickup basketball, did normal-person things. He was no Eustace Conway. But he was closer to Conway than to the average college student. An assistant registrar drove out there and found him. "You might shave and clean up. Coach K wants you at practice tomorrow." Baker played out the year and even saw time on the court against University of North Carolina—Duke's premier rival. The starters were getting embarrassed, so coach put in the walkons. They came back, led by Baker. He nailed a three-pointer, sending the crowd into a frenzy. Heard his name chanted. Made it a ball game again. Then Krzyzewski put the starters back in, and these better-known players blew the game all over again. Baker's name is in brass in Cameron Indoor Stadium as a letterman on that team. Not bad for a kid sleeping in the woods when the season began.

The Perrys like the woods, naturally, so when I visited them in the North Carolina mountains I was not surprised to find that they lived way out in the country.[27] The next valley over was never electrified: "It's called Dark Ridge," Baker said. Their house is 175 years old and 95 percent wood, notched and pegged construction, with handmade wrought iron nails. The Perrys raise goats, chickens, and more crops than they know what to do with. "I just love this farm," Patience recently wrote me in an email. "Eggs with orange yolks and armloads of produce every day. If you lived closer, I would be giving you cucumbers and squash right now. Can't wait for the tomatoes and corn to ripen!" Sounds old-fashioned, a throwback, right? But they also have gravity-fed spring water, a fully functioning National Weather Service co-op station and fiber-optic internet. They have solar panels on their roof, electrifying the place without the grid but with plenty of technology. This is not Dark Ridge. It's a complex mix of high-tech and high-touch and high-ag.

There's no television in the cabin, naturally. And somehow the Perry kids are remarkably . . . normal. They run competitively, play basketball like their dad did, help in the garden and with the animals like their mom does. The family is not against technology. They just live differently. In fact, Patience admits, the kids use screens now that they're teenagers. But the parents collect everyone's devices at 10:00 p.m. The Perry kids will head to college soon, where of course they will make their own decisions. Hopefully the family has ruined them for a life of screens and prepared them instead for a life of face-to-face relationships while growing food and exercising and reading amid overflowing tables.

These things take wisdom and discernment to suss out. Baker grew up a missionary kid in Latin America, surrounded by the violence against socialists, Christian and otherwise, committing him to at least semi-radical politics thereafter. Patience grew up the child of a Catholic parent and a Jewish one, whose families had to learn, wait for it, *patience* with one another. They are among the most worryingly awesome people I've ever met. Patience mentions that menstrual blood is really good for growing the garden. I rethink the plate of kale I've just devoured.

See? Worryingly awesome.

Baker works as a climate scientist in the geography department at Appalachian State University. He's a celebrated academic, an accomplished scientist, and he studies the history locked in the snowfall in some of the highest inhabited places in the world.[28] His work involves some of the most sophisticated technology on the planet—installing weather stations to monitor minute changes at altitudes that try to kill human beings. There are stories to be told in the ice in the Andes and the Himalayas, and Baker aims to tell them. And in a planet on fire, what he learns about the climate may help us all survive. The Perrys may have Luddite tendencies in the home, but there are things that need really sophisticated tools to be done well.

These families amaze me. They inspire me. They don't have the restrictive effect of families that are so awesome you can't approach them. They make me want to join them in community. They make me want to live differently. Sure, they're several steps ahead of any of the rest of us in terms of their commitments to Jesus's beloved poor and planet. But they make me realize I can de-emphasize the phone and Netflix; my kids won't evaporate from the face of the planet without Instagram (their protestations notwithstanding). The Perrys' and the Whites' holiness is a holiness that attracts. It makes me want to come closer—not just to them but to God. I envy their kids. Sure they're poorly adjusted to lots of our technological assumptions. But we need *more* people similarly poorly adjusted. There is life without devices. More life even.

———————

Perhaps it's not shocking that families can be exemplars, refractions of holiness in this way. The first couple in our Scriptures have things pretty good. There is work to do in God's garden—naming the animals—but it is not onerous (Gen. 2:19–20). But Adam and Eve aren't in the garden ten minutes before they're listening to the snake rather than God, blaming each other and the animal God made, and, by implication, God (3:11–13). Adam will now work the ground he came from with sweat, and Eve will suffer through childbirth (3:16–19). It is interesting that these two areas—food production and childbirth—have been made easier for most of us by technology but in some ways murkier, morally speaking. The way we farm is extractive and may be ruining the planet; the way we have babies incurs much less pain and death, at least in the West—though the birth rates in the West lag behind replacement birth rates.[29] Adam and Eve's children, Cain and Abel, offer sacrifices, one acceptable, the other not, and jealousy ensues. In the ultimate act of horror for any parents, their first son rises up and murders their second. The Bible's portrait of human treachery is unflinchingly honest, without a whiff of sentimentality, and unremittingly grim.

Things get worse from here, if that were possible, until God decides to start over. Wipe us all out. Begin with a clean slate. He'll use the best family he can find, the only family that shows much in the way of holiness. Noah and his loved ones are saved on the ark along with enough of all the other animals to repopulate the planet after the flood. The technology involved in shipbuilding is elaborate, to say the least (keeping the hyenas away from the lambs! Imagine!). Not ten minutes after the flood recedes, Noah is drunk, displaying his naked shame, and cursing his own children (Gen. 9:20–27). That Hamitic curse became part of Europe's mythology around Black people, a mythology that helped drive chattel slavery for half a millennium. God's people are always industrious. Joseph rises up to be the right hand of an emperor. And he sets the stage for his own people's enslavement. He builds granaries, hoards produce, makes Pharaoh the lone provider of life in the region, and forces people to give up their lands to beg the government for the grain they once grew themselves (47:19–21).

The problem is never simply "out there," attributable to some villain whose elimination will mean world bliss. It is in *here*, in us. And we can't fix it, not with any tool or device. Technology gives us more of us, more humanity in all its gore and glory. But for all our proficiency in making stuff, we cannot remake ourselves.

So God chooses another way. God will choose a family, one family, from among the whole earth. Not the best family, unlike the choice of Noah. Perhaps the unlikeliest family. Abram and Sarai are old, and they could not have children even when they were young. God's choice draws Sarai's laughter, appropriately. Which nonagenarians are on the waiting list at the maternity ward? Yet God, who made everything in the first place, can surely remake things, like a womb, like the earth, like our lives. Abraham and Sarah do become father and mother to a people more numerous than the stars of the sky or the sand on the shore. And they are God's beloved, God's bride, God's chosen. Not God's perfect—far from it. To read the Bible is, if anything, to see a record of human bleakness. But God promised to remake all things through this one human family. I remember hearing Rabbi Jonathan Sacks tell a story about his children coming to him with the joyful discovery that they had a famous ancestor. "Who?" he asked, a little sore that having a former chief rabbi of Great Britain for a father wasn't ego-satisfying enough. "If you go back far enough we're descended from Abraham!" Right, that's, uh, what it means to be Jewish!

Christians hold that Jesus Christ has grafted us into this family as well. We gentiles are not included by nature; we're snuck in by grace. It is a hard thing to be God's favorite in the world. Just ask our Jewish forebears and neighbors how that has gone for them. But to be part of God's family is to show God's determination. God will stick with his people precisely when we don't deserve it. And God will renew the world through us. Not just despite us, and certainly not for our benefit alone. God's blessings are not *for* God's people. They are *through* God's people, *for* everybody else (Gen. 12:4). God's "solution" to the problem of human evil and intransigence, to the thorns in creation and the thorniness of our hearts, is a family.

This is not a very efficient technology. It seems, by current count, to take millennia. This family is marked by internecine bitterness and bloodshed, illegitimate children and unauthorized progeny, embarrassing stories and surprising grace. But it is a sign that God has something for families to do: be part of his renewal of the cosmos. It is a sign that God means to repair everything we human beings have ruined and he will do this not via technology but through the very human beings who've done the ruining. The surprising choice of Abraham and Sarah and their strange, unlikely progeny might even be a sign that technology itself can be part of God's redemptive purposes. You never know. God has used unlikelier things.

Like human beings themselves.

- What is the most "worryingly awesome" family you know? How do they discipline their use of technology?

- Have you seen technology try to play savior? How do we relegate it back to the status of servant rather than master?

FIVE

Undistracted Friendship

A short passage tucked into the book of 2 John sets the stage for a biblical model of friendship in the digital age. The writer adds a disclaimer to the end of his epistle: "Although I have much to write to you, I would rather not use paper and ink; instead I hope to come to you and talk with you face to face, so that our joy may be complete" (v. 12). He writes this, of course, with ink on the paper in the letter he sends. Yes, the relationship between himself and the woman from a distant church is one made possible only by technology. Is a visit realistic? We don't know. Does he ever make it? Also unknown. But the relationship is as historic as they come—it was, after all, Bible-worthy.

This overtly technological and inarguably biblical method of communication comes with a warning, however: this is not all there is. The communication between two friends, two siblings in Christ, on ink and papyrus is subpar to in-person rendezvous.

When it comes to how digital technology affects our relationships, the façade is one of connection, reliability, and steadfast union. We are able to connect with one another instantly, wherever we might be located in the world. We are always available, no matter the dinner party or bedtime routine that might be interrupted. We are able to maintain a sense of the relationship despite moving away, or even moving on. Of all the brilliant advances in the ways we can connect with one another, this universalizing of availability has changed the way we practice friendship the most.

Behind this façade, the reality of our aggressively connected culture is that relationships are not flourishing. Instead, our culture fosters loneliness and ill-commitment like we've never seen before.[1] We have already used Sherry Turkle's famous work *Alone Together* to express the false sense of relationship we have while our technology is in the picture. Take a bus ride anywhere in your city and you'll see the majority of riders scrolling on their screens instead of greeting one another. It is a common occurrence on one's daily commute to hear the bus driver ask someone over the loudspeaker to give up their seat for a person of different ability—an ask that, for the sake of humanity, we hope wouldn't be necessary had one simply the eyes to notice.

Friendship and relationship trends like ghosting and bailing are prevalent in Millennial and Generation Z age groups. Without warning, someone ceases contact or neglects to show up for an event without explanation or follow-up. Unfortunately, a hearty faith in the Holy Ghost is not enough to keep one from being ghosted, I (Andria) should know. I've been there. These trends cause harm not only to those suffering the injustice of an unexplained slight but to the empathy and humanity of those performing them as well.

The neuroscientist Jamil Zaki goes so far as to suggest that empathy itself is endangered. He attributes this to our modern notions of relationships and the technologies we use to maintain them. In an interview with the *Washington Post* he said, "We see more people than ever but know fewer of them. Rituals that used to bring us into regular contact, ranging from bowling leagues to grocery shopping, have been replaced by more solitary pursuits, often carried out online. The result is our interactions with each other are often thinned out, anonymous and tribal—barren soil for empathy."[2] By being constantly connected we are disconnecting from what makes us human—our ability to feel. Be it by way of information silos that prevent us from seeing news that might make our hearts break or the ability to hurt others without having to witness their suffering, we are avoiding discomfort and vulnerability with our virtual blinders.

We are a fallen people.

Yet the opposite is also true. We only know we are fallen if God is making redemption possible. Heartbreaking news is inescapable if we open our eyes to see it, and compassion fatigue is running rampant among those who haven't had the training to deal with it.[3] Over the past decade the necessity of this kind of technology for relationship building has emerged more clearly, even amid its downfalls. The modern desire to achieve status, success, or financial stability requires sacrifice—and not the biblical kind. What is asked of us is to give up time spent with loved ones, moments lost in conversation, agenda-less gatherings, and last-minute get-togethers. What we gain is time spent doing the things we have been told are most important: working and earning, and improving ourselves so we can do more of both. In a life spent on the go, we take our relationships like we take our lunch breaks—on our way from A to B, briefly, and often through a window (or a screen).

Arguably, however, the technology that enables us to maintain relationships in a world moving as quickly as our Western one is good and redeemable. The desire to remain connected while in pursuit of the good life is noble, hard as it is to "have your cake and eat it too." The intention has never been to do away with friendship, but the harm has proven to be the same when we try to maximize friendship's efficiency. I remember one woman in her early thirties, armed with a baby and mean to-do list, arrived in an online small group declaring, "I don't have time for the how are yous today, but please tell me what I can do to support you."

It's not that we don't want to be there for one another, it's that we no longer have to be in order to still be considered a good enough friend. The cultural pursuit of productivity as a value has forced us to minimize the time we spend together and maximize the time we spend apart. The technology hasn't made it so. Nor has the virus. We have.

The texts and emails and video chats and location trackers have enabled us to check in and out like we're punching a time clock—effectively maintaining a kind of knowledge and awareness of one another but not having such knowledge encroach on our own lives. We made these tools because we felt we needed them in order to be good enough.

But what if Christ alone makes us "good enough"?

In 2007 Steve Jobs gave a famous speech introducing the first iPhone. Cal Newport, the author of *Digital Minimalism*, describes a technological intention far different from where we've landed. He writes that Jobs "seemed to understand the iPhone as something that would help us with a small number of activities—listening to music, placing calls, generating directions. He didn't seek to radically change the rhythm of users' daily lives. He simply wanted to take experiences we already found important and make them better."[4]

How'd that work out for all of us?!

Never had there been more time to think about this purpose versus actual practice than during the coronavirus lockdown of 2020–21. As the world closed the doors on businesses and gathering places and as the respiratory illness swept across the globe, we were left with only one way to connect—our online technologies. We learned quickly that while we would rather not, it would have to do.

This way of connecting in an unprecedented time is not without its dangers. The writer of 2 John tells us of false teachers and of the dangers of acceptance without discernment. Around the world many feared that if screen time was the only time we could have with one another, then it would only make us more screen obsessed and empathetically incompetent. Children would grow longer horns,[5] and people would shun time in nature. Such visions conjured up scenes in our mind's eye from *The Walking Dead* (which we would have all now binge-watched). Thankfully, what happened was the opposite.

Families were taking time away from their work each day to aimlessly walk the neighborhood and smile at every passerby. Playing card games and doing puzzles with one another instead of watching television became favorite pastimes. Reports of people maintaining more authentic relationships and developing brand-new ones in this time surfaced with surprising frequency.[6] In response to a question about her church's Zoom meetings versus their meeting in the pews, one congregation member said that it was nice to not just see the backs of people's heads; instead of only knowing whether someone got a haircut, she could tell when they had been crying.

What a remarkable testimony to how we are paying attention to one another right now. Certainly Turkle's findings in *Alone Together* are correct—our constant connectivity leads us to a place where it seems we are alone together. More than once I've looked up from my phone only to see a dinner table full of friends staring down at theirs. In the time of coronavirus, however, it was impossible to forget the phrase we heard over and over at the start of the pandemic: "together, apart." The statement felt akin to "together, alone." When it became impossible for us to be together, we used all the tools available to us to remain connected. While we quickly learned that it wasn't the same, nor even a close substitute, we were creative and intentional with showing up for one another. It felt like, for the first time in decades, our social tools were being used the way they were created to be; not as replacements for in-person interaction but as supplements to those relationships.

Scripture offers us many models of friendship, most influential for the Christian being the relationship between Jesus and his disciples. From the moment each of the Twelve are called, we see them develop friendships that require trust, commitment, endurance, intimacy, honesty, and physical presence. They also require independence and autonomy. The church has long argued that what we do, we can only do in embodied relationships with one another. Yet our very model of discipleship suggests this will not always be possible. The promise is, and has always been, *I will leave you—and you will continue as if I am still here* (John 14). In the ascended Christ, we experience what it is to be with and be without in the same moment. And in the descending Spirit we are shown what it is we are called to do in the liminal space of the living God: carry on.

For the writer of 2 John, the continuation of this relationship was rife with as many possibilities as the moment in which he could gather in body with the woman to whom the letter is addressed and her church. Joy would be greater when they were together, but the work of the kingdom need not wait for such a moment, nor the relationship suffer because of it. This is the attitude with which we must approach our friendships in a digital age—we use these tools not in place of bodily presence but in case we have to love one another from afar.

There's a sketch by comedian Sebastian Maniscalco in which he describes the ancient emotion of joy upon having someone drop by unexpectedly. He says, "It's a different feeling when your doorbell rings today opposed to twenty years ago. Twenty years ago, if your doorbell rang, that was a happy moment in your house. It was called 'company.'" He goes on to describe the ritual of unanticipated guests, the special hand towels, the cake, the parade of family members, only to conclude by saying, "Now your doorbell rings? It's like what the —?!"[7]

Author and exvangelical Glennon Doyle reflects on the stages of doorbell dysmorphia using the language of grief:

1. Denial: This cannot be happening. ALL OF THE PEOPLE AL-LOWED TO BE IN THIS HOUSE ARE ALREADY IN THIS HOUSE. Maybe it was the TV. IS THE TV ON?
2. Anger: WHO *DOES* THIS? WHAT KIND OF BOUNDARY-LESS AGGRESSOR RINGS SOMEONE'S DOORBELL IN BROAD DAYLIGHT?
3. Bargaining: Don't move, don't breathe—maybe they'll go away.
4. Depression: Why? Why us? Why anyone? Why is life so hard?
5. Acceptance: Damnit to hell. You—the little one—we volunteer you. Put on some pants, act normal, and answer the door.[8]

We are used to the constant interruption of our devices bing-ing and ringing at all hours; we don't expect to be physically inter-rupted. Even that word rolling off the keys of my computer names the shift—not delighted, not surprised, not even mildly amused, but interrupted. Long gone are the days when an unexpected visitor was cause for celebration. Instead, we hide behind boxes of cereal in the supermarket when we see someone we know, only moments after double-tapping their latest Instagram post.

I remember doing a student ministry practicum in a small village outside of London. The dying art of receiving "company" became painfully familiar. It was the person who just "popped by" to see how you were doing. The congregant who "stopped in" to ask you to tea. The woman who saw a new car in the park and wanted to "say hello." It was the unexpected ring of the doorbell and the subsequent internal conversation that went something like, *Who on earth could that be?* knowing full well I had not vacuumed in anticipation of houseguests.

I quickly learned that my desire to be company-ready in the face of personal interaction would need to fade if I wanted to participate fully in the life of the community. On one morning, with the house in particular Wednesday shambles, I confess to throwing myself off a dining room chair in response to seeing a familiar face outside, in fear they might see me through the window, catch my eye, and proceed to want to join me for porridge. I could not be seen like this, in my lounge clothes, with toothpaste still on my upper lip. It wasn't good enough. I wasn't company-ready.

After crawling out of the kitchen, I knew I had some re-evaluating to do. Christ's command to love others as he loved us (John 15:12) isn't a suggestion to keep an endless supply of hostess gifts at hand, nor a call to accept hospitality only when I feel I deserve it. It is a command to appear before God and one another as flawed, knowing grace abounds in those flaws, in ourselves and in others. It is a call to friendship—a letting go of the self and joining another in the journey of their life—a radical welcome, not without flaws but with undeniable grace. I have never attended so many dinners, never steeped as many cups of tea, never paused for so many conversations among the roses with strangers as joyfully as I did during those six months. And I have never seen the face of Christ more clearly. What was initially an interruption became nothing other than an indulgence.

———————

In their 2016 book *The Distracted Mind*, Adam Gazzaley and Larry D. Rosen explore how this constant state of interruption has also changed our expectations of one another in our relationships.[9] Technological advancements leave little room for us to be unreachable, and the constant demands on our attention are exhausting us right out of our friendships. Gazzaley and Rosen explain that unlike the answering machine, which was meant for telephone communication that someone would receive when they returned home for the day, the text message, email, or social media post anticipates an immediate acceptance and response, often eliciting anger, frustration, or hurt when an immediate response isn't given. Instead of giving our friends or colleagues the benefit of the doubt, or at least the courtesy of a day to themselves, we engage in dramatic imaginative feuds and overthink what we did wrong, all because of a slow (read: reasonable) response time.

We long for the intimacy that such a commitment to one another fosters, but the constant notification spiral of our devices isn't enough to do it. These high-maintenance relationships with impossible expectations aren't as multidimensional as they would have us believe. It takes work to be in a real relationship, and our technology has given us the permission and wherewithal to simplify and make our lives easier. We are life hacking the life right out of ourselves.

The "life hack" phenomenon took off several years ago with tips like "The hole in your pot handles is so that your stirring spoon never needs to touch the countertop!" and "Did you know there is a hidden knife inside the lid of a Nutella jar to cut open the sealed container top?" How about that one-minute mug brownie? Life changing. But this process of hacking and scything is not making our lives any less full. Instead we want more—more tips, more tricks, and more time to immerse ourselves in the world we are only just discovering thanks to Google and those Facebook videos that play before you've even clicked on them. Simplify? Sure, but I'll have to tell Susan I can't hang out with her. Marie Kondo is on and I didn't realize how much of a hoarder I was. We are, as Gazzaley and Rosen write, too distracted for friendship.

William Deresiewicz takes this one step further in an article aptly titled "Faux Friendship" by asking, "Are our friendships now anything more than a form of distraction?"[10] Trust the Facebook generation to turn "friend" into the most passive verb imaginable. It does not suggest action, conversation, giving, or selflessness. Instead, to "friend" someone now means to notify them, in the midst of whatever they were doing, of your willingness to be publicly associated with them. Oftentimes this is as far as the relationship goes, lest a nudge or a poke inspire a deeper conversation about how it would be good to grab coffee "soon."

This "soon," of course, is the same amount of commitment as the dreaded "maybe," which—as musician Jack Johnson sings—"pretty much always means no."[11] Our ability to prioritize our relationships with one another over the distraction of the email lottery pull or the blinking notifications on our screens is falling drastically short of good enough. The good news is that we can put practices in place to ensure that those we gather with get our undivided attention. The bad news is that gathering in the first place is getting harder and harder to orchestrate.

As people who look to the ancient text of the Bible for an understanding of modern life, it might make sense to turn to Aristotle in the Facebook age as well. The classic philosophical understandings of friendship can shed light on our current circumstances. For Aristotle, friendships belonged to one of three categories: pleasure, utility, or mutuality.[12] The first two categories of relationships were time limited, existing only as long as the relationship was useful, desirable, or easy. Dubbed "accidental," these relationships were more a product of convenience than anything—think the coworker you work out with, the neighborhood mom you have coffee with on the street corner, or the fellow student you spill intimate details of your life to on the steps outside the law building. It is uncomfortable to hear the majority of our relationships so appropriately described with such a harsh word ("accidental"), yet of the hundred, thousand, or five thousand friends you have on your social media pages, how many have you had to take an extra moment with to remember how or where you know them from? "Accidental" seems only fitting.

A relationship based on mutuality and respect for each other's values and virtues, on the other hand, is fit to last a lifetime, in part because these relationships take time to cultivate. Such friendships, unlike the neighborhood gab group, arise not out of necessity or convenience but out of careful and compassionate consideration for each other's value, and they serve not only me, here and now, but also the world that witnesses them.

Surprisingly, the slowly cultivated friendship that is lost in our world of McRelationships is one that our most-recent technologies can re-teach us. According to leading research in the areas of emotional AI, what makes robotic companions so good at their jobs is the way they take time to learn our individual ways of being in the world and adjust or correct their responses based on the newest knowledge. This is, perhaps, why the positive response to such technologies suggests that people feel listened to and understood. In essence, they are. But it is not that our robotic companions do so better than we ourselves do. Again, technological friendship is not a replacement for humankind; it is an enhancement.

In her exploration of these kinds of relational AI technologies, Rana el Kaliouby argues that human beings have been "bonding with nonhuman objects since long before computers and AI."[13] She mentions the relationship a young child might have with a doll or blanket as being an essential part of how we learn to care for others, or the less-healthy attachment an adult might have with a special car or other toy. Society has never expressed a fear that the car or the action figure might replace a desire for human interaction, and similarly we need not fear that our love of Amazon's Alexa will replace our love for the friend who shows up when we are most in need.

But this is the crux of the matter—if we hope to use our technologies as the tools they should be instead of the rulers we fear they are becoming, we need to let them re-teach us how to show up. It is a lesson the church could stand to offer. Relationships are what we do, even here, even now, especially so. The slow, consistent, sacrificial nature of what it means to build friendships with one another is a biblical model for a world in which human flourishing requires that we stay rooted to one another, not to the tools that enable us to be everywhere.

In the book of Ruth we see the fruits of such a relationship. Upon the death of Naomi's husband and sons, Naomi encourages her daughters-in-law to return to their own families that they might not be foreigners in a strange land. Ruth, upon hearing Naomi's invitation, clings to her and pleads to stay, pledging her life in six ways: that she will go wherever Naomi goes, stay whenever she stays, love her people, love her God, die with her, and be buried with her (1:16–17). This is a promise that Apple's Siri could make without so much as a moment's thought, but could we?

Ruth roots herself to Naomi, sacrificing belonging with her own people for a mutual love that will serve to protect and provide for both women through all life's seasons. The two women risk a vulnerable existence as widows. Ruth knows that leaving Naomi alone will risk her mother-in-law's chances of survival. So, she stays. And she not only stays but works: she gleans the fields as an outsider; she lessens herself before another so that her friendship with Naomi will thrive. But where there is sacrificial love, there is God. Ruth's noble efforts eventually draw the attention of the owner of the fields, Boaz, who condescends himself as master to Ruth the outsider so they can marry, thus securing Ruth a place in the messianic lineage as mother to Obed, King David's grandfather.

This is not a model of friendship we see represented well on social media. Instead of rooting ourselves to those we love, we invite them to pad our ego. Every "like" is only an opportunity to showcase ourselves, what we might be able to offer, or what others might have to contribute to our lives. These public declarations of acceptance overshadow the more faithful friendship that simply whispers, "I am here with you. What an honor it is to support you."

The friendship in our social media feeds is about personal display. Unlike Ruth's selfless promise to remain with Naomi, the friendships we count among our Facebook followers run the risk of being all about us. Deresiewicz writes,

> Now we can see why friendship has become the characteristically modern relationship. Modernity believes in equality, and friendships, unlike traditional relationships, are egalitarian. Modernity believes in individualism. Friendships serve no public purpose and exist independent of all other bonds. Modernity believes in choice. Friendships, unlike blood ties, are elective; indeed, the rise of friendship coincided with the shift away from arranged marriage. Modernity believes in self-expression. Friends, because we choose them, give us back an image of ourselves. Modernity believes in freedom. Even modern marriage entails contractual obligations, but friendship involves no fixed commitments. The modern temper runs toward unrestricted fluidity and flexibility, the endless play of possibility, and so is perfectly suited to the informal, improvisational nature of friendship. We can be friends with whomever we want, however we want, for as long as we want.[14]

Whoever, however, whenever. A long way from Ruth's six-tiered commitment to Naomi. We fear dictatorship and prefer a powerful showcasing of personal whims. It sounds like a display—which is perfectly fitting, considering the platform it likely exists on: one akin to a storefront window in which the mannequins enjoy a beautifully plated and plastic Thanksgiving meal in the perfectly staged linens of the most recent Fall line from L.L. Bean. We are not, as we have already established, our most authentic selves online. Instead, we make-believe and hope that someone also playing dress-up sees through the mask just enough to glimpse something that sparks familiarity. It is, as Aristotle said, an accident.

These accidental friendships serve their purpose if we return to calling our social sites "networks," as they were dubbed in the early 2000s. Each passer-by has an opportunity to look into our store window and decide for themselves if they would like to consume what we are offering. If they would, we have ourselves a customer—a business deal, a potential client or partner, a new person in our network. But we aren't arguing networking can be done online (it can), we're arguing that discipleship can be (and should be). Following Christ is not a posed display of all that is wonderful and sinless in our lives, attractive enough for the outsider to want to be like us. It is a demonstration of how throughout our lives we answer again and again the call to follow until, finally, we are like him. Our friendships could use much the same posture.

The ease of online technology for those of us who know how it works has made us too impatient to demonstrate anything. A display we can handle—we were doing it anyway—but to demonstrate something requires the ingredients we have been chronically short of: time, consistency, selflessness.

One of the tasks of the church when the most recent global pandemic shut down our buildings and made it impossible to meet in person was to figure out how to continue being together despite having to be apart. The answer seemed obvious—the church would turn to online technologies. This was a simple solution for urban ministries, Millennial pastors, and youth groups, as it was one that already existed. The challenge of the mainline church, however, was that those it primarily served in its in-person iterations were of an older generation, one that did not use words like FaceTime, Zoom, or Skype, let alone know how to use the platforms themselves. What would be required of the church, in the coming days, weeks, and months, would be a demonstration.

Meeting our people where they were at required demonstrating how it worked. Pastors spent hours a day on the phone to senior congregants talking them through how to watch YouTube. Practice meetings were set up so that ministers could walk through how to use Zoom for when the actual meeting rolled around. Youth leaders learned new technologies when their workday ended so they could painstakingly walk their participants through the technologies the next day so their parents didn't have to. I heard of one congregation who paired its teens with "church grandparents" and arranged phone calls to answer any technical questions they might have.

For a generation that has opted to answer the how-to questions with "just Google it," this time of change for our communities required that all demographics slow down, develop a patient disposition, and look at things from a different perspective. The result was a sense of amazement. Not only did the technologies make sense, but they made life easier, more meaningful, better.

For a brief moment, when the novel coronavirus began requiring us to exist inside our homes and without one another, the way we had trained ourselves to communicate became novel as well. Virtual game nights and happy hours popped up, online murder mysteries and dance clubs emerged, and grandparents who had never before used the tech came to cherish video calls with grandchildren. The technology we had at our fingertips was a wonder and we wondered if we had been taking it for granted.

Congregations met one another face-to-face in online coffee times and choir rehearsals. Gordon, a ninety-year-old man at his first online church event, burst into laughter as he accidentally cloned himself three separate times on the screen. He commented, "I was hoping I'd be able to sneak in under the radar to my first online event, but now it seems there are three of me!" An intimidating feat accomplished, he is now known and loved by more members of the church than before.

"I woke up this morning," he said to the group that was gathered, "and realized it was never going to get less scary. . . . And today felt like a good day to do something scary." A blessed demonstration.

When we are ready to show up for the other—as Ruth was for Naomi, the pastor to her congregation, Gordon to his community— we begin the journey of biblical friendship. And whatever tools it takes to maintain such a promise—a willingness to commit to working the fields, the capacity to trust a new way of being together, the courage to act in a new way—are holy. They enable the work of Christ in the world; they are a support for the weary hands and feet of the people of God.

In the middle of the pandemic, a local minister was approached to do a wedding. It would be small—five people—allowing it to happen within the health guidelines at the time. The minister, the couple (Jennifer and Denis), and two witnesses would gather together in person for the ceremony, which would be livestreamed to the family and friends who, for safety reasons, couldn't attend in person but who wouldn't miss it for the world. The wedding was unique for many reasons, the pandemic being one, but the piece that stood out for those who watched and for the minister himself was the Scripture choice. Jennifer and Denis decided to have read the story of Jesus washing the disciples' feet (John 13), and in response, they would wash each other's feet as a symbol of their commitment to each other and to the gospel.

The act was one of selfless intimacy, and for the close to four hundred people watching the wedding online, it was one of remarkable tenderness. The gusto with which the congregation of friends and family responded "We do!" in the chat box when asked if they would do all in their power to support and uphold the covenant between the two was made possible by the sharing of this sacramental moment. Given the tools to witness the union of these two individuals meant that not only the couple was blessed but the friends were too, by the gift of Christ incarnate in that moment.

The wedding had been planned to take place in person, and the foot washing would have been beautiful that way too, but the promise these two made to each other need not wait, and with technology being as it was, the couple didn't feel the need to postpone. In a conversation I had with her online, Jennifer said, "We found a creative way to honour our relationship to God and others, despite some roadblocks. It is our hope that this principle will help us in our marriage as well." She continued to say that while there were fewer people than imagined and no reception, they ended up with more friends witnessing their union than would have otherwise been possible. Folks from Russia and England joined in the promise to walk with the couple and, as a bonus, Jennifer stated, "We are both introverts so in some ways doing it [this] way took a lot of anxiety away. It turned out to be a very intimate ceremony."[15] Not only would it have to do, but it did do, and the friends virtually present saw with their own eyes a life together being started anew.

It is no accident that the language used in Ruth's promise to Naomi is akin to a marriage ceremony. The friendships we have and hold most dear are those within which intimacy is revealed as a covenantal practice. In the Gospel of John, friendship is the result of bearing no secrets (15:15). Christ declares that he and the disciples are not master and servant because they have been witness to all that has been made known to him from God. This form of knowing and witnessing can be done with more ease today than ever before—the technology at our fingertips makes it so.

But when it comes to friendship, ease does not make things easy.

In a book on digital culture, you might expect a chapter about online pornography. We had one, in fact, but decided it didn't fit. This book is about embodiment in every aspect of our lives in a digital age. There are many Christians for whom web porn is a problem. So it has, if anything, been over-discussed in Christian responses to digital culture, especially in evangelical settings. By contrast, more mainline and liberal Christians respond to pornography by pretending it doesn't exist.

What would be a better approach?

Perhaps reading the Bible. The Song of Songs, a friend says, is highly erotic and not at all pornographic. Ancient Jews and Christians forbade young people from reading it, but that may be exactly the wrong approach. There is no need to be squeamish about these glorious and awkward body parts that God gave us with which to love each other and make more people. The Song shows us what these usually covered protuberances are actually for: God loves us ecstatically. God goes out from (ek) any place of statis to love us in the flesh of Jesus. Christianity is an erotic faith: we wash feet and baptize people in the nude (and you thought the ancient church was prudish) and eat and drink our Savior and become so ecstatic we babble incomprehensibly and shout for joy. Sarah Coakley likes to say that Freud is exactly backward: talk about God is not repressed talk about sex, but rather talk about sex is repressed talk about God.[16] So a culture awash in porn is actually full of (quite confused and pitiful) longing for God.

The problem with web pornography is that it is not erotic at all. Its self-gratifying nature shrinks our world, requiring nothing costly from us, objectifying both the viewer and the ones viewed, reducing everyone's humanity. Naomi Wolf points out that for many young boys, "real naked women are just bad porn."[17] I remember a high school anatomy teacher apologizing for a sketch of a splayed-legged person that no one wanted to look at: "Sorry, this isn't very . . . romantic." For generations now, web porn has been our sex ed teacher. What would a better one look like?

Desire depends on an interplay between veiling and unveiling, a glimpse awakening deeper longing, a giving over of oneself and not just taking, as we see in the Song. We're rarely fully satisfied, always longing for more, and often left just short of what we think we want. No wonder the Bible uses marriage as an image for Christ's stormy love affair with the church. In this life, our longing is occasionally satisfied, mostly not, prying open in us a desire for another sort of marriage altogether. One day, in a promised coming consummation, all longing will be satisfied unendingly, as Jesus comes to marry us, his bride, at last.

I (Jason) remember a friend in my fellowship group in college described how she prayed (this is the sort of exciting tête-à-tête I had as an evangelical back then). "I feel God filling me. Moving around inside me." Then she looked at me: "I'm not unaware how sexual that sounds. It is." But it wasn't at all pornographic. It induced longing from me, not for her but for God. I wanted to pray like she did. I still do. That's what sex is for—to give us a glimpse of just how good prayer can be. And prayer exists to hasten the day when humanity will be entirely filled with God, who will one day fill all creation like the waters fill the sea.

Distance, accessibility, illness, or time constraints no longer mean we cannot fully arrive, if we choose to use our tools in this way, but using our online tools in this way is not common. Instead, generations of people showcase only what they want people to know and see, and thus they control content with firewall-like security. When friendships are maintained only in these online spaces with such vigorous controls around sharing, it becomes impossible to develop friendships that honor the biblical models set before us.

To preach these kinds of friendships in the digital age is to remind people that there is a difference between being vulnerable and being vocal, between being seen and being known. Watching others live their lives is not the same as witnessing to the life being lived. To show up is to warm the water in the basin and sit at the feet of one another, taking turns washing and drying and anointing, as if to say *I am always here, but right now, I am only here.*

And when, for reasons beyond our control, we cannot show up with the basin ourselves, we can show up to witness with the same intention, sacrificing time and attention for the sake of another.

Our virtual tools are designed to make everything more efficient, but our human right as those who have created these tools is to learn how to use them as we best see fit. For days in the office, the ability to multitask and respond quickly might be exactly what we need, but for time in virtual conversation with friends, our tools might require different parameters.

One group of friends in Vancouver has covenanted to turn the "self-view" off on their Zoom meetings so that they can look one another in the eye instead of looking at their own reflections.[18] Another group has formalized the way conversation happens: instead of letting the energy of the room dictate where conversation goes, they give each person in the group formal time to share what's on their heart. These kinds of adjustments are exactly what are required of us if we are going to use technology to enhance or maintain our real friendships digitally. Much like the way worship changed when we couldn't meet in person, the way we hold space for one another needs to shift as well. A text message is not good enough when important news is shared, and silence is extra awkward when there's a time lag.

Unfortunately for us, John's fifteenth chapter has more to say about what friendship means than a baring of one's soul. "No one has greater love than this," Jesus says, "to lay down one's life for one's friends" (15:13). It is not enough to show up for one another if there is no action that follows. Like our call to discipleship and the verb "to friend" should imply, we are not merely to display friendship but sacrificially to demonstrate it.

During the first month of British Columbia's imposed COVID-19 quarantine, it was a common occurrence to see people posting screenshots of virtual friend get-togethers on their social media pages. Images of smiling faces lined up on the screen became as prevalent as those at restaurant tables only weeks before. What these images displayed was a solidarity of experience and a commitment to getting through a challenging season together. What they lacked was a demonstration of authentic support.

Instead, several local churches began updating their social media pages with a simple offering: We're all in this together, but some of us have it easier. Tell us what you need and we'll get it to you. A demonstration. The great toilet paper shortage of 2020 was a small frustration for many of us, but for those with limited mobility and resources, it was a health and safety crisis. Game nights were nice, but a hand sanitizer delivery service was better.

Let's return to Deresiewicz's comment about friendships simply being a distraction: it took a while for the quarantine blues to produce anything other than sheer entertainment. But as the pandemic continued, we settled into what life would look like for a while, and and we realized our relationships could be healthier for it. With a deeper understanding of what in-person gathering meant for our friendships, we chose to look forward to meeting together in person again, and yet, before that time, we used the tools we had for more meaningful connection.

Small group ministries flourished because large congregations lacked the ability to gather but had the resources to place people in more intentional groups. Those who may otherwise never have met, let alone become friends, began meeting with regularity to discuss the circumstances of life that didn't stop because of a rampant virus, to lift one another up, to support each other, and to pray. These friendships forged in a time of virtual necessity were neither accidental nor utilitarian; instead, they were intentional relationships governed by a demonstration of willingness and accountability.

To lay down one's life for a friend these days might not mean the same journey to the cross of Christ or the promise and commitment of Ruth to Naomi, but it is something of a sacrifice to leave behind the pull of productivity and the fear of missing out for an uninterrupted moment with a friend. It might mean ringing the doorbell unexpectedly, or at least answering it, whether we are company-ready or not.

What friendship looks like in this digital age is nothing unusual for the Christian. It is a conscious effort to arrive, foibles and all, to the place where love is demonstrated not because it can be seen but because it simply is. What a friend we have who is not only there but present—rooted despite all the chaos of our own making, demonstrating the promise to stay when everything is calling us to ghost.

- How has your oldest friendship (or a relationship you have had since pre-texting days) been changed by fast-food forms of communication?

- Confess to a time you let technology do the heavy lifting of friendship for you (ghosting, texting a last-minute cancellation, claiming you "didn't receive the email"), and play through how an embodied approach might have altered the relationship. What would have been different?

- What biblical model of friendship do you aspire to? What role could your smartphone play in it?

SIX

The Internet Is (Kind of) a Place

The instructions were simple: "Go," he declared, "and make disciples of all nations" (Matt. 28:19).

Dumbfounded on the mountain, they stood, waiting for more. A heavenly bestowal of power perhaps, a Mosaic staff that would enable them to heal, a knighting of divine courage to ensure they would never falter, anything! "Go . . . baptizing them in the name of the Father and of the Son and of the Holy Spirit," he continued, "and teaching them to obey everything that I have commanded you" (Matt. 28:19–20).

Christ's Great Commission is the manual template for brevity, giving the disciples one task: to move from the place they currently stand into places unknown, sharing with all the good news of Jesus Christ risen from the grave. The instruction is not a suggestion or a guideline. It is a command—and one that has the potential to answer all our questions about how we do digital ministry well. The internet, with all its residents, is a mission field. It's time we go there and make a few disciples.

Throughout the history of Christian mission, Christ's parting command to the apostles has often been forgotten. Among Protestants, it wasn't until the eighteenth century that a redefinition of "disciples" and "all nations" formed what we now consider to be the missional imperative. The English Baptist minister and missionary William Carey wrote in his 1792 *Enquiry*:

> It seems as if many thought the commission was sufficiently put in execution by what the apostles and others have done; that we have enough to do to attend to the salvation of our own countrymen. . . . It is thus that multitudes sit at ease, and give themselves no concern about the far greater part of their fellow-sinners, who to this day, are lost in ignorance and idolatry. There seems also to be an opinion existing in the minds of some, that because the apostles were extraordinary officers and have no proper successors, and because many things which were right for them to do would be utterly unwarrantable for us, therefore it may not be immediately binding on us to execute the commission, though it was so upon them.[1]

A Millennial refrain rings through the air: "You only had one job!" Carey's concerns still haunt corners of our denominations today as numbers in many of our no-longer-mainline churches continue to decline. What good is feeding the hungry if we can't feed ourselves? "We have enough to do!" we insist. And certainly, we do. Many of our denominations are facing foundational changes in polity, structure, and governance in response to the decline of congregational numbers and financial contributions, my own (Andria's) no exception.[2] The fear that focusing missional attention outside our own denomination might take away from the familiar and meaningful work of the church is warranted. Yet a commitment to new and experimental ways of ministry and mission is mandatory if we are to continue to follow Christ's uncomfortable call to "go and make disciples."

Despite declining numbers, much of the work being done to facilitate Christ's new world in the twenty-first century tells a more hopeful story than the one Carey despairs over. A story in which the churches of the Reformation recognize their own need to reform again in the ways in which they proclaim Christ alive. Around the globe and across denominational divides we see innovative explorations of what communities of faith can look like reaching out into the world.

The Church of England's Fresh Expressions movement, started in 2004, and the United Church of Canada's EDGE network are only two examples of how redefining mission can enliven the body of Christ to seek out the lost sheep and encourage connectivity where there were only ruptures. These networks exist to help support and fund both a re-imagined church and faith-inspired justice in this moment.[3] Evangelism 2.0.

To be certain, there is no time stamp on Christ's declarative sending forth. "Remember, I am with you always, to the end of the age" (Matt. 28:20), he comforts (or menaces) us. The church through the ages has certainly continued to travel where the sandals of Christ never did. The disciples immediately were tasked with something else, something more, something different. Surely, our discipleship in this age is no different from this, calling us beyond the self-imposed borders that might hold us captive and instead into all the nations.

Today, the commission to make disciples of all nations cannot exclude the nations we ourselves have created in an attempt to fulfill the emptiness of a culture that has oversold the joy of individualization. In her book *Blessed Are the Consumers*, Sallie McFague states, "We have been living as 'misplaced persons' for several centuries; it is time for us to come home and rejoice in the comfort that only home can give."[4] To expect that the modern world will experience a prodigal moment based on our invitation, however, is an illusion. To encourage others to come home might require a bolder invitation than the one that the church has been extending, and technology just might be the key.

As someone who self-identifies as a cradle-Christian, my (Andria's) progressive Protestant upbringing gave me a surprising number of resources for dodging this commission à la Carey's eighteenth-century conviction. In theory, mission and evangelism could be avoided if one spent enough time in service and spiritual discernment—a path I spent twenty-five years walking before tripping over a rogue root of praxis one day on my Twitter feed.

In 2012 a marketing professional and entrepreneur by the name of Sandi Krakowski tweeted a link to a message she claimed to be inspiring. Inspiration was something I was lacking as an early-twenties college dropout, so I took the clickbait. I was desperate for a nudge, and she happened to be there. What I found on the other side of the link was not the self-promotion I expected but instead a sermon by North Carolina megachurch pastor Steven Furtick, titled "Don't Stop on 6." This message was the beginning of a journey back to a God from whom I hadn't realized I had turned away. It was also the beginning of my own climb up the mountain of discipleship. The relevance here, as we talk about new ways of being the church in the world, is that while Furtick's message of resilience and perseverance (based on Joshua's battle at Jericho) spoke to my circumstance on a surface level, it wasn't the message itself that re-focused my eyes on Christ. It was the medium.

I had stopped attending weekly worship in 2011 after a particularly dramatic exit from the city in which I lived tied to the usual quarter-life crisis culprits: relationships, restlessness, and resentment. Never having read the Scriptures closely enough to see myself in them, I was convinced there was no place for me. Instead, hundreds of kilometers away from my community, my shame and I rented an illegal loft above a coffee shop that sold pot brownies before they were legal, and I began freelancing puff pieces for an internet newspaper. My faith remained intact for a short while as I tried to hustle an understanding of grace, but it quickly faded into the smoke that rose from the grates in the floorboards when no one from the church came looking for me. I was the sheep, lost in the wilderness, not unwilling to return but unsure how. Until one day, a stranger's voice broke through the noise of the internet and said, "Come to church."

The church I wound up in was not like the ones of my youth. There were no vestments, no processions, no Lord's Supper, certainly no flying buttresses. Instead there was a computer screen, someone welcoming me with a TSN-quality performance,[5] a worship experience pertaining to me and me specifically, and a man rocking a serious fade telling me I was in the right place, that I had been found. It didn't take much, but that was more than enough to lead me home.

While Furtick's style of theology and worship didn't parallel my own (I was, after all, about as liberal a Christian as they came, raised on "Draw the Circle Wide" not "Come to the Altar"[6]), I found myself captivated and encouraged by the presence of such an enormous community of Christians online. The resource had never been made known to me by my own people. Instead, a woman from Phoenix, Arizona, found me among her 200,000+ followers and, with 280 characters, led me directly back from whence I came. Commission completed, Spirit embraced.

My relationship with an online version of church began here. For several months I searched for churches that might be a closer denominational fit for me, churches that were broadcasting high-quality worship and offering online faith formation, support, and virtual community. I wasn't unwilling to show up in person, but I saw value in the immediate accessibility of a place that was at my fingertips no matter where (or when) I was. I wouldn't have walked into a church on that July day in 2012, but I happily clicked on one.

Not finding exactly what I was looking for in my search, I returned to my home congregation armed by an encounter with the living God, a heart of repentance, and a new sense of call: to create a place online for those like myself, who yearned to be discipled, with awareness of the complexity of the path in today's world. To take the message of God-made-human to *all* nations at once seemed a necessarily simple instruction to me: go there.

Over three billion people are using the internet, searching for something (often *anything*). What could the church offer them?

———

According to an article published in WIRED in 2018, if you were to visit the town of Huntington Beach, California, you would find on the waterfront an inconspicuous RV park. Inside you would be greeted by travel trailers of all the normal variety—Airstreams, teardrops, Bolers, pop-ups—and one thirty-foot Apex Ultra-Lite that houses a man named DJ, his family of four, and their Virtual Reality Church.[7] This church is, according to DJ, the first of its kind. Ex-pastors of a megachurch in Pennsylvania, DJ and his wife launched this new church in early 2018 and now preach and preside over a virtual service every Sunday, welcoming guests from all over the world. DJ says this church is very similar to attending a service in real life, apart from the occasional glitches—for example, someone might all of a sudden appear to be missing a limb, or a glitch might prevent someone from getting the timing just right on a song.

While DJ's church might have been among the first of its kind, that technology has placed us here is no surprise. For more than twenty years theologians, ministers, and professionals of all fields have been working hard to imagine what the future looks like, online. Philip Meadowsi describes this as a natural part of our "anthropomorphic" identity.[8] As creatures given dominion over creation, it is natural that we wish to use our power to create and master all we can within that creation. The idea of having the freedom to create our own reality is the stuff metaphysical dreams are made of. Our sight, second to time itself, is one of the greatest illusions we have. It is no shock that humankind—those created to create, shaped to shape, and loved into loving beings—somehow inhabited the desire to do more with all of it, to fashion the world according to what we see as its maximum potential, to create something that appears to be "as good as it gets." As Helen Keller is often quoted as saying, "The only thing worse than being blind is having sight with no vision."

The Millennial generation is often critiqued for being entitled in this sense, for wanting to one-up the divine, biohack their way to immortality, and life hack their way into the infinite. More accurately, however, they are simply impassioned and have been encouraged to take their one brief cycle of existence on this earth to a different place—one of imagination, innovation, unparalleled potential, and above all else, service. Confront a North American Millennial on a street corner with a quote from Mary Oliver asking what they want to do with their "one wild and precious life"[9] and they will tell you they seek to find their purpose, however religious (or not) they think they are. In other words, they seek to find the thing they were created to offer to the world or, in the language of discipleship, to be of service.

But to be of service in this kind of world has societal implications like never before. Our immediate relationships are not our only sphere of reach. One does not need money or inherited status to reach beyond the boundaries of geography and influence the lives of others. The only thing one needs to have is a decent signal.

Rich Villodas, the pastor of New Life Fellowship Church in Queens, whom we spoke about earlier, is a shining example of how social media can be used to reach beyond one's immediate circle of influence. New Life Fellowship is a congregation that, on Sunday mornings, comprises more than seventy-five different nations. They are a culturally diverse community of engaged and enthusiastic Christ followers, but Villodas doesn't let his pastoral care and proclamation stop there. Over the past five years he has been developing a personal "philosophy of engagement"—an intentional way of using social media in which he remains the pastor but to a much larger, worldwide congregation.

Learning early on in his Twitter usage that amassing large numbers of followers means less freedom to speak thoughtlessly, Villodas now weighs his words carefully, saying, "I don't just preach on Sunday mornings, this is another platform for me to proclaim."[10] He frequently asks himself how to speak truth into the world in a pastoral and priestly way and uses his own daily devotions as an additional effort to encourage and uplift those who might find him on his Twitter platform.

With all this reaching out, however, our society has seen a form of separation anxiety emerge. The line between our embodied and disembodied realities has blurred to the point where we no longer have access to all aspects of our lives. To be "fully present" is a perpetual battle of attention. Am I of service here, in this moment, within this specific circumstance, or am I present online, where the service could, potentially, have a greater impact? Am I more fully myself planted here in this neighborhood, or is my authenticity in fuller bloom behind my Facebook posts? Are my needs being met more completely by the uncomfortable practice of asking for what I need from those around me whom I love, or are they being repressed and camouflaged by the hit of dopamine I get when a new like comes in? This constant need for more of *everything* is the brink of an existential crisis without a philosophy to guide it. It is an ongoing pressing of the question, How can we maximize our personal selves to experience more fully the abundance of this life when we are, in fact, existing as multiple selves?

These questions and longings of the Millennial generation and increasingly other, less stereotypical demographics, represent the landscape in which church leaders are being called to pastor. Whether you respond to this with a like or with a sad-face emoji, the landscape matters for how we approach this technological neighborhood. Our single responsibility is our understanding of these questions and our views of how to gather the wandering in an effort to shepherd them toward the reconciling nature of Christ, through whom all things are made whole. This landscape is not an optional adventure route; it's the only way forward.

Villodas sheepishly tells a story of receiving a gift of Catholic prayer beads from a congregation member. Skeptical at first, he soon found the beads to be a helpful tool not only in prayer but in presence. "Walking around I'm tempted to pull out my phone and walk and text or walk and tweet," he says, "but now I hold these prayer beads and say the Jesus prayer instead!"

These contemplative practices have much to offer us in the form of technological management. "Digital detox" is commonplace language now for going a certain period of time without one's phone or even just an app, but our ancient practices of fasting could have hinted toward the success of such an undertaking. Villodas doesn't limit his screen time, but he acknowledges that he has good days and bad days. He laughs. "I usually get my weekly screen time summaries on Sundays during worship and this . . . is a great time to ask for forgiveness."[11]

The challenges of discipleship in this moment of the reign of Christ are not for the faint of heart. While we can make light of our pitiable shortcomings, we too recognize what Villodas identifies as a fragility of soul. For decades we have struggled to define our cultural context as it stands in front of us now: postmodern, post-Enlightenment, and primarily post-Christian. It seems once again that the church—at the very least its Westernized iterations—is being called to redefine the cultures from within which we live our lives of faith in hopes of finding a way to share the ever-relevant Word of God with those who would be better for it. Lesslie Newbigin, in his early work on mission, insists that it is not our place to "explain the gospel in terms of our modern scientific culture" but rather to "explain our culture in terms of the gospel."[12] In other words, by approaching the territory of online technology as one where we can meet the searching and the lost, we can speak the gospel into our culture in a way that continues to both surprise and challenge us.

Who could dispute that postmodern Western society thrives on a consumerist mentality and value system? While economics is certainly at play here, the tendency to consume is not solely influenced by capitalism. Instead, we are a generation of North Americans who are, quite unassumingly, raised by their surroundings to be hungry and never to be satiated—in life, in possessions, in money, in love, in power. It is, then, no surprise we find ourselves also a culture within the confines of post-Christendom. The Scriptures stand countercultural to what our actions profess we value. The choice between what's offered by this world versus the riches of a new one is ours to make. However, Generations X, Y, and Z are not devoid of desire for an encounter with the Divine. In actuality, the longing of these generations who are classified as post-Christian or primarily secular is very much in alignment with that of generations past. A life, as Paul writes to Timothy, that really is life (1 Tim. 6:19).

––––––––––––––

Recently, at a gathering of the West Coast spiritual-but-not-religious crowd for a talk on compassion, a local New Age leader, who wore yoga pants and sat on a velvet meditation pillow, began a session with two rhetorical questions: "Hey Vancouver, whatever happened to church? Where is the place we go to process the darkness in community so we can let the light back in?" It was apparent in the provocative *mm-hmms* and *wows* around the dimly lit room that meaning-making and community-based living were collective values that were currently unmet. Though my (Andria's) hand remained down like an anchor, the hunger to do an altar call right then and there was voracious. Religion cannot be separated from the media we participate in. The stumbling block, however, is that we Christians have often tried to do just this.

To be clear, for more than a century Christians have been using new communication technologies to bring people into the church. The results have always been mixed. In the 1920s radio preachers were accused of using the "devil's tool"[13] to get new membership and later, in the 1950s, television evangelists were similarly condemned for using "on-stage chicanery" to take advantage of those in "desperate circumstances."[14] *Send us your money and we'll save your souls!* Nowadays, Hillsong Young & Free trucks their synthesizers and hype-people into arenas to win over the faith of America's teens through dance music. *Buy our praise albums and your kids won't bump and grind!* But this brave venturing into modern machine has indeed brought thousands of people into contact with the stories of Christ—people who otherwise might never have put themselves on a corresponding path.

The difference explored here is not whether technology has been utilized by the church as a whole, for it has. The question is whether the church has bothered to consider its online evangelism "real" mission. Does its mission extend past the stage of proclamation and into the realm of teaching, does it respond to human needs through service, does it transform unjust structures of society, and does it represent the kingdom where the integrity of creation is renewed?

Kerry Karram has been attending church via an online broadcast since 2015, around the same time I was hired by her congregation to explore what the church could do differently online. Kerry, a middle-aged woman of sparkling humor with a vibrant capacity to serve selflessly, and I bonded over a shared sense that online worship had the potential to become "real church," as opposed to just a live feed of someone else's worship experience.

The first time we met, we talked for hours over Skype. We spoke of online church not only as an avenue of evangelism, hoping to one day introduce strangers on the internet to the community of people in the pews, but also about how online worship could be a tool for creating deep, lasting relationships in its own right. This online church could shape people in real formation, whether or not they ever walked through the doors of the building. Whenever we spoke there was a great urgency in Kerry's tone. She was adamant that we were on to something, and her tone of voice conveyed the hopeful edge of someone who had a wildly fantastic idea that had only just started to percolate. Could it be, she seemed to be asking, that my form of worship might actually count?

Perceiving to be "on to" the internet is a testament to just how behind the times our places of worship are. Around leadership-board tables worldwide, meeting agendas still house items like "Communications: Do We Need It?" and "Projector: Is the One from 1993 Still

Working Well Enough?" Technology and the church don't seem to mix. And yet without it, we wouldn't be here.

As we've already said, much of how we do church at all is founded on the letters written by the apostle Paul early in the first century. Paul, a church-planting evangelist with an exemplary zeal for Christ's commission, stops at nothing to assure Jew and gentile alike that all are invited into the promise of the coming kingdom. All nations, remember.

With almost half the world's population using the internet,[15] ignoring technology is no longer realistic. The internet has become a place, not just a thing. What is troubling is that this place appears to be broken. The internet is no longer being used because it's helpful but because we are helpless. We are trusting the turmoil of our souls to the algorithms of machines. *Fill us, fix us, find us!* The idolatry of data is arousing us from the contemplative bore of the human experience and encouraging us to lessen ourselves to the stimulation of its mechanics.

More troubling, perhaps, than the idolatry of a place we cannot see, hear, touch, taste, or smell is the thought that such a place might be revered as sacred. For millions of users around the world, the internet is not just a place one occasionally drops by to pick up the odd thing when the pantry runs dry; it is the well at which they drink.[16] The third place.

This language of "third place," popularized in the early '90s by Ray Oldenburg, refers to a location outside of home or work where members of the community gather to be in relationship with one another.[17] Churches, parks, clubs, libraries, and community centers have long been considered the standard third places. *Cheers* introduced a bar as the third place for its cast of characters. *Friends* fans will recognize Central Perk as the coffee shop that housed many major conversations for its characters. These places provide opportunity for newcomers to be welcomed and regulars to know and be known.

As a church, however, there is a vast difference between what we offer in this space and, say, what is offered at a Jamba Juice store. Not only are we offering community, but we are offering a covenantal relationship between us and the living God, a relationship that is housed and nurtured within the church community. This relationship is profoundly incarnational. The way we embody our faith and our love for one another is unique. To suggest, then, that we move our faith from a place of flesh and bone into an abstract environment feels heretical. And yet we tell the story of life after the body's natural end so well. What is there to fear in the pursuit of offering people the story of resurrection in an environment that so badly needs it?

Being the church, wherever we choose to do so, is more than just the worship that takes place on Sunday morning. We must offer opportunities to meet others, chances to engage with learning and growth, the prospect of healthy change and transformation, occasions for eating together, playing together, and supporting one another. As a Christian place, we must offer opportunities to serve and follow faithfully and to grow in love for one another and for Christ. This is the pastoral opportunity of approaching an online environment as a new location for genuine communal engagement. In fact, we already do these things all the time. The internet is one more place for us to offer the welcome that marks healthy parish life.

Kerry was seeking for herself this third place—specifically a church. She was looking for a church where she could arrive and be met with more than just words on a screen. She wanted an invitation to join in a way of life. What makes Kerry unique in this search is that she was only looking for this place online. Kerry will not attend a church in person. She suffers from a social anxiety so severe that to visit her beloved congregation, ripe with attentive and welcoming people, poses a serious threat to her health.

An experience in early 2015 set Kerry's heart racing over two hundred beats per minute as she sat in the back pew of Highlands United Church. To return, she fears, might kill her. Through no fault of her own, or of the church, Kerry was ostracized from a community she longed to be part of. She would call the community her home, but for lack of resources and imagination, the capacity of the congregation to include her was limited to sixty minutes, within those walls, once a week, and even that was gone.

In those early conversations, the slow move toward an online church community that could rival an enfleshed gathering was exciting but frustrating. The resources for high-end technical equipment and competent staff weren't budgeted for. The invisibility of an online congregation made them easy to forget. The sustainability of upgrades felt like an endless loop of software notifications, and the complex nature of new platforms left more things broken than working on any given Sunday. Kerry's feedback was immensely valuable, even amid its discouraging critique: How could she experience the hubbub of coffee hour? Where was her invitation to give online? Could the announcements also reflect events that weren't localized? Why wasn't the sound working? How could she find out who else attended online? What was she supposed to do with herself during the passing of the peace? What about Communion?

The invitation in Kerry's frustration was a righteous one. How can someone with a physical limitation still take the Christian community up on its offer to accept and welcome if that welcome requires showing up bodily? It was also a challenge: What prevents the church from leaving the safety of our sanctuaries and stepping into new places—broken places—knowing that our very job is to proclaim redemption into the broken places of our world?

In his 1970s manual for the future, Alvin Toffler articulated a collective anxiety brought about by an accelerated pace of cultural change.[18] His industry-breaking insight—that we must adapt like never before if we want to experience the future like we once imagined it—sparked a new onslaught of change theories, ones that sought to articulate the devastation of society if we were unable to keep up. What was a dramatic approach to the human condition fifty years ago has only since intensified with the emergence of individual technologies and a corporate economy. Not only are our people unable to keep up with the mere demands of everyday life, but the planet is falling apart, its resources are dwindling, our capacity for empathy and authenticity are waning, and trust in this thing we call church is wavering at best.

The need to adapt to our context, to match the speed of the world around us, is no longer a slight suggestion or uncomfortable stretch but an uncompromising demand; it is a bursting tear that is leaving the body permanently marked by the pain of its own incapacity. And yet, in this wound is an invitation into a visionary kind of discernment. How are we to be Christian in this version of the world? For it is no accident that the miracle of God's call is to be answered here and now.

Not much puts the fear of God into a mainline minister like being told that their sermon is about to be livestreamed. We immediately wish we were sharing some other news—news with fewer implications, news that didn't have to do with souls or Spirit or a slain Lamb. Sharing news like *this*, on *the internet*, well, we don't know about that.

Alternatively, if you inform your neighborhood evangelical that the broadcast platform is down this Sunday, you might find him running for the hills. How can we save people if we can't reach them? If a preacher preaches and no one records it, was a word really given? Surely if Grandmother can upload another accidental selfie, the good news of Christ can find its way into binary code!

These two distinct camps bracket a wide-ranging set of opinions surrounding the use of technology in the church. From clip art on PowerPoint to electronic conversions, the ways in which we communicate the gospel vary, but we can agree on one thing: we do need to communicate it. From Gutenberg to Google, that much hasn't changed.

The desire to bring the transformative story of Christ into the world in innovative and relevant ways is a holy one. The question we're asking is how we separate that desire from the ones of our own flesh—the ones that have us creating content for new followers, sermon titles for Twitter, electronic liturgy for Millennials. At what point does the good news become our news, not for the life of the world but for its likes?

Soliciting a buy-in to the Christian faith as if it's a commodity is problematic. While it might work on paper (true, a good marketing campaign can get more people in the doors), grab tactics can result in a lack of proper formation and risk shaping a faith that is fabricated and not properly founded on Christ. It is also reminiscent of a colonial mission laden with false power and authority.

But if it is not to preserve ourselves, idolize ourselves, or to draw in a crowd, what purpose does a faith founded on physical relationship have in virtual space? Why should we pay people to run social media accounts, train volunteers on camera angles, or register for a Vimeo account if what matters most is the community we gather with, in the flesh?

Our participation in new media is not something we should do out of obligation to remain modern and visible. This is part of it, but only at its most surface level. The more meaningful utilization of these media is to shape and disciple people, like Kerry, who are living a loud existence of Christian expression outside the church walls.

It is true that Kerry will not come into the sanctuary she loves on Sunday mornings, but when asked recently by another member why she no longer attends church, her response was quick and simple: "I do." And this church encourages her to be of service in the world and in relationship with those around her. Small groups are comfortable for Kerry. On a Thursday evening (pre-COVID-19) you would find her in the kitchen of the church, cooking meals for those who attended the weekly dinner. You will find her in Bible studies, asking questions and listening to those around her. You will find her in coffee shops with other church members talking about life and God, and throughout all of 2017 you could find her on Sunday mornings leading a group of seniors through worship as they gathered to participate in the church broadcast, remotely.

It is not only mental health concerns, however, that prevent people from joining congregations in person. Shut-ins at Amica Seniors Centre in a Vancouver neighborhood showed interest in attending weekly services but were unable to manage the logistics of mass transportation and health aides. Instead, equipped with an order of service, lay leaders from the local church community, including Kerry, would visit and facilitate the gathering of mobility-challenged elders in prayer and song, taking them to church but not outside the safety of their required care provider. For many of the volunteers, this experience built a confidence in lay leadership while also allowing them to grow deep relationships with those they would have never otherwise met.

Kerry's eyes well up as she lists the names of people in the congregation she has met because of the opportunity to serve with them through the online ministry. "I am so grateful" she repeats over and over. "And so were those to whom we brought the church. Some of them thought they would never go again."

In Thunder Bay, Ontario, the congregation of Trinity United Church gathers for worship on Sunday mornings like many other communities of faith. Rev. Dr. Randy Boyd welcomes those who have joined the broadcast on livestream, along with two other congregations that will be sharing in the leadership of the service that morning. Over the course of the service, each church plays a liturgical role, with leaders from various locations being projected into the other sanctuaries. This ministry of technology, at least in rural Canada where the geographic distance between rural congregations makes it nearly impossible for one minister to have multiple charges, has saved the lives of congregations that otherwise could not afford to stay open.

Illness, relocation, travel plans, incarceration, limited resources, remote habitation, learning challenges, health concerns, and human preference are all reasons people cite as attending online church communities over embodied ones. For many people, attending these online churches is done in their own small communities like the examples listed above, but for others the experience is and will remain a solitary one. It is into all of these circumstances that we are being called to speak the Word of God as completely as we can, in knowledge that the resurrected Christ can speak through us whether in person or online.

About a year after Kerry and I began our conversation around the online life of this particular congregation, she discerned that she wanted to become a member of the church. The covenantal relationship between herself and the people with whom she was on this journey was important, as was the knowledge that she truly did belong to a place. On the selected Sunday, at the selected moment, Kerry received a phone call from the lead minister who proceeded to put her on speakerphone in front of the congregation.

"Do you, Kerry, promise to journey in community with this congregation in accordance to its values and follow the ways of the living Christ?"

"I so promise."

"And do you, the people of this congregation, promise to support and uphold Kerry in her faith journey?"

"We so promise."

In this promise, new life is groaning its way into existence. The ascended Christ, who is with us always even to the end of the age, continues to send us to places beyond our wildest imaginations.

Our social media platforms and online church broadcasts prove we can proclaim the good news with gusto and ferocity. Christians have been able to teach, respond in support to those in need, and organize to confront injustice. But a community of catechetical and sacramental importance is missing from our virtual existence. Instead of treating our online church followers, our Facebook followers, and our Twitter followers as cyber blips, could we look at them as potential fellow disciples? Could we see them as true followers of the risen and reigning Christ? If the challenge is, as it has always been, one of reach and accessibility, then the solution is, as it has always been, mission.

So much territory is still unknown when it comes to the possibilities of our virtual existence. This ground is the setting of both dystopic and utopian literature. How we are to navigate such a realm is complicated. A secular *Washington Post* article in the early '90s gave it a good shot. David Nicholson wrote, "The more technology invades our lives, the more it obscures the real issues—the fact that our lives are really about love and work and death, about creating and maintaining relationships that sustain us, about finding meaningful vocations, and about living with the knowledge that, alone among all creatures, we know one day we're going to die. Technology may affect the material conditions of our lives, but it hasn't done much yet for our souls."[19]

This is debatable thirty years later. Relationships have been destroyed over unhealthy internet habits, our ability to memorize phone numbers has lapsed, and our attention spans can hardly manage a Netflix loading screen. Not to mention research on the loneliness and depression epidemics that suggests this internet stuff is just making it worse. Our souls might not be in peril (we can agree to disagree here), but a person can no longer argue they haven't been affected. Despite all this, the brave leaders who endeavor to take to the platforms have more than enough cheering them on. As we bring our ancient technology—the Bible—to the new, it is important to remember we do not need to adapt the message, only the way it meets our attention.

To presume we will find God at work in this place—this virtual, disembodied, unknown place—is to have faith that our being sent out as disciples is good enough. To go, expecting the tools of our Scriptures are enough. This belief itself is countercultural to our consumer nature. Yet, as Nicholson so eloquently wrote in his op-ed, what people are truly longing for is not something shiny and new but something ancient. They're looking for love, comfort, meaning, and relationship—things the missionally minded can introduce, no matter the field.

While much debate has taken place over the incongruous relationship between an embodied faith and a disembodied culture, one only has to revisit 2 John 12 to know that the gospel does not stop at the place where our feet cannot wander.

To be a missionary one must first extend the invitation to hear. When the apostles sought to teach and connect with communities far away, they penned letters and sent them, despite the epistles not being the ideal circumstances for gospel delivery. Our job as sent leaders in a church that is still desperate for a missionary approach to faith is, according to J. Andrew Kirk, to "persuade a generation, whose identity is tied up with the urge to consume, that increasing acquisitions are an illusory reflection of the good life that is reflected in the anticipated messianic banquet."[20] How we live our lives in all our cultural environments is a testimony to the *missio Dei*, the working of God in the world. To watch carefully for the movement of God in our complex, powerful, and human-made environments and ask how we can best be disciples within those contexts is where we, the church, are called to next.

While the understanding of mission need not change in order to do mission in a virtual environment, there are differences from some of the classic views that make this particular field unknown territory. With the ability now to create entire identities that do not reflect our embodied reality, the distinction between public and private is increasingly difficult. The hardest part of starting an online ministry is knowing who you're reaching! Avatars are cute, but they're not an introduction.

However, as we discussed regarding identity in chapter 2, complete privacy these days is unrealistic. Whether intentional or not, our core values cross the border between public and private every time we log on and click "like." We might not know who exactly is watching, but we know if they've been moved because they'll come back, they'll "like and subscribe," to borrow the popular YouTube language.

What this means for the internet as a mission field is that there is no hiding, either as missionary or as convert. Meadowsi writes, "The virtual world offers limitless connectivity. There is no doubt that digital media are enabling us to be more connected to others. Indeed, immersion in digital culture is the experience of being pervasively connected to everyone, everywhere and always."[21] By being in constant community (defined here as in the virtual company of others), our witness truly is taking place every waking and sleeping moment. Those who have joined us online, anonymously or otherwise, are leaving one online space and moving into another. And they will take us with them.

In his work on mission in the twenty-first century, Darrell Guder writes, "The church of Jesus Christ is, and has always been, clearly visible to the observing eye."[22] However, we have seen a place within our culture that deserves more missional attention if this is to continue to ring true.

"I had no other options," Kerry tells me, "and this online community brought me in. It has the ability to bring in the lost." To be seen, Kerry reflects, is to be found. As someone living with Post-Traumatic Stress Disorder (PTSD), Kerry makes an analogy. She mentions therapy dogs, often suggested to people struggling with PTSD or social anxieties as a tool for helping normalize daily life in companionship. Kerry does not have a therapy dog. "I could," she says, "but what would it offer me? Unconditional love. Support. Safety. Well, I get that from my church."

Through questioning and learning together, through suffering and sharing together, through endeavoring to make a change, and through the practice of reaching out to others with the good news in faith that God is working where we have not yet been able to go, people's lives are being redeemed. Not only that, the space itself—this vast, boundaryless, virtual space—is being redeemed.

The fleshed Christ in our midst is not one who shies away from the unsavory facets of a particular age or culture but one who points and says, "There—go there, to all the nations."

- What is the online experience of your church? Take the time to attend one of your online services (if you have one) on a Sunday you have off. Do you feel like a participant or an audience member?

- How does your congregation continue to welcome people into life together after your initial hello and "here's our program brochure"? Is there anything online to suggest that this continued way of fellowship exists?

- Think back to the most meaningful encounter you've had online—perhaps one that sparked a real relationship or that changed something for you. What made it so tangible?

SEVEN

Virtual Virtue

Can Christians celebrate the Eucharist online?

The question seemed more hypothetical before coronatide. COVID-19 forced us to forego meeting together in person. Businesses and churches and educational institutions shifted our worship and study online, with mixed results. Zoom and other digital conferencing technologies are marvels. But they are profoundly unsatisfying. They show the great gift it is to be together in person—one we take for granted. Those of us in the new "information economy" were surprised to learn that being together in the body still matters. Profoundly.

Not long after physical distancing changed our lives, churches began to ask the question above. Can we ask parishioners to dash to the pantry, come back with something to eat and drink, and call it Communion? An answer requires clarification: What sort of Christians are we talking about? There are Christians for whom worship is always eucharistic. Catholics, Orthodox, some Anglicans and Lutherans—anybody of a sacramental bent—tend to say the sacrament can only be celebrated in person. They might broadcast the celebration of the sacrament by a priest, which can indeed convey grace, but no pantry dash, please. Catholics, for example, often gather for Adoration. They kneel in the presence of the consecrated host, usually displayed in a monstrance, like the sun and its rays

(Mal. 4:2). They don't consume the sacrament on that occasion. They pray in the bodily presence of Jesus, the "prisoner of love," in pious descriptions of such traditions. Physical distancing means we cannot commune, but we can pray in the presence of Jesus without communing. Traditions that lean (or run!) toward the real presence of Jesus Christ in the Eucharist tend to frown on any virtual celebration of the sacrament. The whole point is that Jesus gathers a people, like his Jewish forebears around the Passover, like his gathered saints at the eschatological banquet at the end of all things. You can't transmit water or bread or wine through a computer screen. Don't try. To "commune" without the physical sacraments is to succumb to the Gnostic tendencies of our digital age—that is, the belief that embodied reality is a problem to be overcome. Orthodox Christian faith says our bodies are our glory. God is fleshed in the body of Jesus and shares himself in bread and wine to divinize our bodies. Whatever computers are good for (and Minecraft is a fine thing), don't pretend they can convey sacramental grace the way *actual* water can, the way bread and wine do. The push for salvation sans mediation is just Gnosticism. A heresy. Don't do it.

Lower-church Protestants pretty quickly said we can indeed commune online. The pastor would ask participants to plan ahead or, failing that, to go to their kitchens and come back with bread and wine or juice. The pastor would lead the celebration of the sacrament, as usual, and all would commune. Those left distant from one another during a plague are thereby brought close, made one. The body of Christ is always a virtual body. All the angels and saints gather around this table. There are always more people present than can be seen with our physical eyes. The church around the world gathers in that moment. The body of Christ extends unimaginably beyond mere physical proximity to a single table in one church building. There is nothing magical about the pastor's prayers any more than the prayers of any other baptized person. Any follower of Jesus can ask Jesus to be present in this meal and expect him to meet them there. The home is no less holy than the church. In fact, this can be an opportunity for Christians to realize their homes are places of worship, not just places to eat and sleep and stream and store stuff. The eucharistic table overflows space and time to include all of our places of work and play, and to include all creation eventually. It would be odd to commend a eucharistic fast just because we cannot be together in person. Christ has no trouble being present to each one of us in any time and place. Why not hallow the home where he meets us, the humble food and drink through which he promises to be present? Or even recognize he has *already* hallowed them. The New Testament does not obviously demand a priest for any of this to work. And even if it does, Christ our High Priest is never absent or unavailable, nor prevented by plague or pestilence from being bodily present with us (Ps. 91:6). And baptism makes us all priests. Not to allow Communion online is to give in to the worst hierarchical reduction of discipleship to an institution. We used to break out our worst polemic for such claims ("priestcraft," "whore of Babylon," that sort of thing). Go ahead. Commune at home. It might even save you.

Both of these visions have theological strength and pastoral appeal, and both have clear weaknesses. They show our ecumenical fault lines. Do we need a priest for . . . anything? Does ordination or baptism make a priest? Is Christ "really" present in the Eucharist, and what do we mean by "real"? What do we mean by "Eucharist"?! If a layperson substitutes chips and soda for bread and wine, does that prohibit Christ from being present somehow? If more Catholic emphases threaten a kind of institutionalization or even bureaucratization of grace—we clergy protecting our turf—Protestant emphases threaten a Gnostic reduction of humanity to individuals and our perceived psychological needs.

Perhaps the real miracle is that Christ is head of a body so fractious as this. And yet he calls us one! God came among us in flesh to say that. I (Jason) want to argue, then, that we should celebrate the sacraments only when gathered in the flesh. Andria will object below. For me, faith should be as tactile as God determines to be in Mary's womb.

———

This series is about phases of human life and what Christian tradition says about each. To be human means we are born, we join a family, we struggle with addictions, we live with disabilities, we strive for justice, we get sick, and eventually we die. Yet the incarnation says there is glory precisely in our lowliness. Oh, and we use tools. Some of those tools take on the contours we call "technology." They are a marvel. Each of us carries around in our pocket a computer with greater power in it than those that flung people to the moon. We need never be geographically lost or without connection to others or without a calculator or flashlight or video game again (these are not all of equal importance, granted). The tools are so remarkable, in fact, that they are changing who we are.

From where we write, we are waiting for a technological salvation. From where you read, gentle reader, such salvation may already be at hand. We await not only testing sufficient to avoid illness or the best possible health care if we catch it. As we write, we await a vaccine; upon its arrival we will trust it will be entirely safe and not cause new ills. We want to be cured entirely of this plague. We assume that will come. COVID-19 will be removed from its role as a life- and economy-destroying pestilence, and we will be able to go about our business, more or less. The lessons we take from the coronavirus will, hopefully, linger among us, though we ought not be overly optimistic—human memories are short. During quarantine, we have had to forego the things that make life worth living in order to stay alive: worship; parties; gatherings for theater, music, or sports; meals with friends or strangers; recreation.

Remember going places? Doing things? Yeah, that was cool.

When God's people are commanded to remember the Passover, we are told that *we* were slaves in Egypt. Not our ancestors. Not some other people a long time ago and far, far away but *we* (Deut. 15:15; 24:18). When Jesus invites his disciples to take bread and drink wine in "remembrance" of him (Luke 22:19), the Greek *anamnesis* is stronger than our associations with the English word "remember" ("Oh *yeah*, I remember that!"). A good translation might be "experience anew." We are there at the table with him. He is the host. The church is his body, so he is also the guest. He is also the *food*. When the Bible commands that we remember, the "we" is a multigenerational, multilocational command. It makes a new body out of atomized parts. Remember—because we human beings are instant forgetters—and nothing is ultimately wasted in God's economy.

We often ask technology to play a role it should never be asked to play: divine savior. Give us life, lest we die, O scientists. Even after our high priests of life and death found a cure, we realized, *Uh oh, there will be other ailments.* We are mortal creatures. We are right to avoid physical contact so as to spare disease from the older and frailer among us. Life is a profound good with unplumbable depths. But we are wrong to expect technology to cure every ill. It is a marvel, keeping us alive, granting us food and transport and health and safety in degrees that human beings in most eras would hardly have been able to imagine. We can see why folks might be tempted to worship it. In theological terms, technology often carries its own eschatology. A false eschatology. A claim that a new era has arrived, a dawn in which we can be liberated from all that ails us. No—only God does that. Through a cross. His kingdom is here but also not yet, and it is no reprieve from struggle. One of the constant struggles in Israel's Scriptures is with idolatry. People are always mixing up Israelite faith with that of their neighbors—building poles on high places, worshiping and sacrificing there. Good kings in Israel do not tolerate the idolatry and cut the poles down. We are worshiping creatures—cut down one pole and we erect another. The God of Israel says no. Only YHWH is worthy of worship. No other god can save.

This is why Scripture gives us practices with which to avoid idolatry. The Sabbath is one.[1] The command to observe the Sabbath and keep it holy is oft-repeated in Israel's Scriptures. There is a reason. It is often neglected. One would think the most-repeated command would be the prohibition against murder or adultery. No. It is the hallowing of the seventh day. Consider the list of the commandments in Deuteronomy 5:1–21. Most are repeated, bullet-point style, without elaboration. The prohibition against idolatry and the commandment to honor the Sabbath receive elaborate explanation. No other gods, even if they are worshiped by family or seem more effective in bringing the results to prayer that you want (vv. 8–10). And honor the seventh day; do no work (vv. 12–15). And not only you but your son, your daughter, your male or female slave, your ox, your donkey, your livestock, and the resident alien in your town. This is not rest for the heads of household alone. It is for the animals and the stranger, the slave of whatever gender. It is a little year of jubilee, once a week.

The reason is clear: "Remember" (that word again!). "Remember that you were a slave in the land of Egypt, and the LORD your God brought you out from there with a mighty hand and an outstretched arm" (v. 15). The Sabbath is rooted in the basic, bedrock saving event of God's action in the world. Judaism makes—no, Judaism *is*—the following remarkable claim: the only God there is intervenes in history personally, to free slaves.[2]

Other versions of the command to rest are rooted in the Lord's own Sabbath rest after having created (Gen. 2:1–3). In Deuteronomy 5 it is rooted in liberation from slavery. Egypt's economy included no rest. Slavery means you are your work. You must never stop. Israel's economy includes regular, promised rest, from the highest to the lowest, the top to bottom of human and animal society alike. Creatures are not made for work but for worship. Some of Israel's neighbors had codified laws showing that workers had to pay owners if they fell ill or otherwise could not work.[3] They did not belong to themselves. That's what slavery means. Their rest deprived their owners of labor, so they paid. Israel's people and animals and even strangers belong not to themselves or any human owner but to God. They can count on regular rest and a share in the bounty of the land.

Christians have an uneven relationship with the command to remember the Sabbath. About the worst Sabbath violator in the Bible is one Jesus of Nazareth.[4] He flouts Sabbath rules as an eschatological announcement: the age of rest and bounty glimpsed on one day in seven is here in person in him. The resurrection of Jesus is such an epochal event that it knocks the calendar off its axis. The day of rest moves, like a sea shifting after an earthquake, and it becomes the first day, the day of resurrection. Christendom codified Sabbath rest from the days of Emperor Theodosius in ancient Rome until about the 1960s. When Christians could no longer prevail on legislatures and chambers of commerce to close businesses one day a week, and blue laws fell into disuse, we gave up on Sabbath altogether. It's as if we said that if we cannot mandate a Sabbath legally, then we won't have one at all. The last generation or two has reminded(!) Christians just how Jewish our faith is supposed to be. We are "a counterculture for the common good."[5] We need not legislate for our non-Christian neighbors to be forced to take a Sabbath (from movie theaters and liquor stores?!). We need to celebrate Sabbath rest ourselves—if we do it right, our neighbors may notice and join in. The quality of our day of resurrection rest will be a witness to our neighbors of the goodness of God. A slew of books and stories on the Sabbath (usually ignoring Jesus's own Sabbath flouting) have reminded us of this. We must be Sabbath people again.

This is God's great gift with which to resist the false eschatological claims of technology. One day a week we turn the devices off. That should extend, of course, to a week a year, or more. Just as work does not define our existence in the Bible, so too technology does not define our existence now. God alone does. Sabbath rest can overflow its banks in other ways. Andy Crouch suggests that we practice prayer before devices come on.[6] Time with God in the morning comes before time on social media. He suggests that we resist the allure of the "glowing rectangles" by arranging our home so that the television is not the center of attention in the main gathering space.[7] If we decide it's okay to have a television or computer screen in the house, then put it in a place where it is awkward to gather. Fill the main living space with, say, musical instruments. Sit there, enjoy one another, talk. And *sing*.[8] Only recently in human history have we had access to near "perfect" music by professionals, leaving all the rest of us feeling unworthy to make any music at all. But music is meant to be participatory, a gift to join us together and to God. Churches singing together may be our most countercultural-for-the-common-good practice. What do strangers in our culture know to sing together? "Happy Birthday"? "Take Me Out to the Ball Game"? "God Save the Queen"? The national anthem? (It might be wise to keep a hymnal around!) Sing together, it will join you to one another and to God.

It may be hard to live life without devices at the center of our lives. At first anyway. We are glued to them. They make so much of our lives so much easier. That is their gift and their curse. Most of the good things in life do not come easy. Musical skill certainly does not. Friendship does not. Love does not. Discipleship does not. Crouch points out that the thrill of a long run can only be accomplished by hard work—there is no shortcut to serious training, just as in discipleship. There are no apps for these things. But we keep thinking there is, seeking the things that really satisfy with a "godlike swipe of the finger."[9] Becoming the sort of people we really want to be requires hard work, discipline, community. The first act of hard work is to turn the devices off. A friend just took up this Sabbath practice and found himself in deeper, richer, and more joyful conversation, doing more cooking, and communing more with nature than he had in years. "I can't wait till next week," he said. Shabbat shalom.

But if technology is often a form of idolatry, surely we should say no to it altogether, not yes to it the other days of the week. Christian critics of technology often sound like it is a sort of essential evil, to be resisted at all costs. They don't mean this or they wouldn't be writing on computers or promoting books on social media. The rhetoric sounds as if the advent of technology is itself the fall narrated in Genesis 3. Before or without technology, we are God's beloved creatures, stretching toward glory in Jesus Christ. After or with it, we are condemned to the Sheol of near lifelessness. I exaggerate. But only a little.

The problem is, human beings have always had technology. We are *homo faber*, the animal that makes stuff. Other creatures use tools, certainly. But we can build on our toolmaking over generations to remake creation itself. This is part of the mandate God gives us in creation—to steward the earth, to oversee its fruitfulness. One recent critic of technology, our neighbor Craig Gay of Regent College, points to the *pre-modern* technologies with which we still have not caught up morally. Writing is a premodern technology. Gay passes on Eric Vogelin's argument that only with ancient Judaism's notion of revelation, of God addressing human beings, calling Abraham out of Ur of the Chaldees, summoning Moses and the Israelites from bondage in Egypt, could we have such notions treasured by moderns as individual personality, responsibility, and agency.[10] Only with written Scripture and with a God who takes agency do we have notions of personhood. These are good things!

Fast-forward a few thousand years, though not yet to modernity. The Protestant Reformation reacts against Catholic teaching that priests and monks and nuns are more serious about faith than anyone else among the baptized. Luther and Calvin insist that any human profession can be one that glorifies God and takes part in God's re-demption of creation. Why should a certain subset of people think their work is special, set apart, *better*? The notion is not biblical, the Reformers rail against it, and suddenly a priesthood of Protestant believers are set loose on the world. The work of any baker or cleaner or clerk is as holy as any priest. This epochal shift lets loose a massive amount of energy directed toward improving human society as an implicit mandate in believers' service to God. The famed Protestant work ethic is born here—if all work is holy, offered to God, it must be done in a manner befitting priestly excellence. Calvinists wouldn't let the individual priest-believer be sure of his or her election to salva-tion. But that one could throw herself or himself into their work as a consequence of their belief, coming as close to "proof" of salvation as is possible for people. We have been worker bees ever since, and we continue to be long after explicitly Protestant faith has passed from the scene. Calvinism is a hard habit to break.

Within this revolution lay hidden an unanticipated, subsequent rev-olution. The charge the Reformers leveled against Catholic orders—why do *they* think *they're* special?—was soon leveled against religion itself. Modernity was born partly in societies writ large making the move against Christian faith that Protestantism first made against Catholicism. The Protestant work ethic, once born in believers show-ing their elect status by their diligence in secular work, became the capitalist work ethic. As modern people, we are all taught the creed "we can be whatever we want, if we put our mind to it." This is false mythology, of course, but it is official state religion now. The crushing burden it places on us is that how our life turns out economically dem-onstrates our actual worth. This is calculated without regard for how much we started with. Those who wind up wealthy usually started that way (in the devastating burn, they "start on third base and act like they hit a triple"). Those who start with nothing feel that it's their own fault, and worse, their neighbors agree. Modern secular culture has delivered gifts to humanity, no doubt. But it was born within the church itself. And like a number of other premodern technologies, we have yet to catch up with what it all means, morally speaking.

A Mennonite teacher of mine (Jason's) took to lamenting technol-ogy in class. We thought he was complaining about his smartphone.

Eventually he made clear that he was speaking of the alphabet. It is a marvel. There is no going back on it. But we still haven't recognized the devastation it has wrought. How much more nuclear energy?!

One of the key markers of modern economics is a radical disjunction of means and ends. Gay's teacher, the great sociologist Peter Berger, pointed out that a worker on an assembly line can spend all day on one of several tasks that will eventually build part of a car. Or she could spend all day on the same task for a part in what eventually becomes a nuclear weapon. Capitalism wants our work to be value neutral. It increases productivity not to have workers standing around asking awkward questions about the fruit of their labor (let alone expecting to share its rewards equally).

This disjunction was itself born in the Middle Ages. William of Ockham and John Duns Scotus had philosophical reasons to uncouple means and ends. The philosophical school they birthed—nominalism—suggested that our language does not naturally "hook into" the reality it describes.[11] Our words are arbitrary. We ascribe them to this or that, but there is no reason to think that words *really* relate to the way things are. Nature was denuded of meaning. Creation became mute. Ever thereafter, "the natural world would cease to be either the Catholic theater of God's grace or the playground of Satan as Luther's *princeps mundi* [prince of the world]. Instead, it would become so much raw material awaiting the imprint of human desires."[12] If you think that language is arbitrary, then it is no more than an imposition of power. Means and ends are divorced. We start hurling around the postmodern accusation that anyone claiming anything is just making a power play. These claims are not novel or sexy postmodernity. They were born in mistakes made by monks in late medieval monasteries.

People today think it's "natural" that their children can do whatever they set their minds to, that nature is so much raw material for our use, that no one sort of person has any more dignity or worth than any other. Those ideas, whatever truth they may contain, have a history in Christian theology. They are bastard children of Christian thought. And they have wrought ill in the world as well as good. Our current digital revolution, for example, leaves us all in a continuous state of partial attention. Our world's best minds are not curing

COVID-19 or cancer or climate change—they're selling advertising to us online.[13] Silicon Valley has so duped us that we all work, unwittingly, for Facebook, Google, Instagram, and other tech and media giants, gleefully handing over oceans of information about ourselves for no compensation. Israel's economy of freedom, of sharing in the land's bounty, is undone. We don't even know that we're slaves, bringing our own straw to the kiln in the form of information about, even pictures of, our children, our spouses, ourselves, our travels, our likes. Technology's promise to make everything easy sounds good. But it undoes the discipline and boundaries that grace anything *worth* having or doing. The gods in our pockets never stretch us to do the hard work of becoming more human, more loving, more joined to the widow and orphan and stranger. They encourage us to curate a mendacious portrait of ourselves on social media, all the while hawking us stuff through that same social media. The devices are designed to give us a charge of dopamine every once in a while, like rats randomly rewarded in some experiment. How many times a day do we check those devices? And what have *we* become, anyway?

In our little corner of the world there remains a lively debate over online theological education. There is a reason some theological institutions, like Regent College, have resisted online education, until coronatide. Regent believes that Christian faith is embodied, incarnational. So we must meet face-to-face to learn its treasures. There is wisdom there. COVID-19 may challenge that wisdom, as Regent and other like-minded institutions have thrown their work online. But its suspicions may be dramatically confirmed. Zoom is a poor substitute for life together in the classroom, the meeting room, the chapel, or on the streets. Gay's book ends with a rousing rendition of praise for creation, for the God who superintends it all, who becomes flesh in Christ to rain down superabundant life on all creation. In order to be truly human we must return to these core beliefs and say a resounding no to technology's false promises.

Of course, there is also a reason some schools (like ours!) have embraced virtual learning even before this crisis. Not as a substitute for in-person learning but as a supplement to it. Learning online is not as good as being in the classroom with people. But it is better than nothing. "In person" education can mean someone turning up late and flustered from her day job and leaving early to pick up her kids. Or he is hardly present, even if he is bodily, not having done the reading or rested enough to stay awake. Online education can include mindful presence and diligent hard work. Further, digital education represents a commitment to the local. We do not ask every student to quit their job (often the very ministry that sent them to seminary in the first place), uproot their family, and move to one of the most expensive cities in the world to study theology. Rather, they can remain where they live, try out what they learn IRL, and deepen their ministries and relationships. In this (tiny! narrow!) sliver of life, a good in-person activity can be stretched to be a still-good virtual activity. It is not the lone example.

Gay's book *Modern Technology and the Human Future* relies heavily on critics of technology such as Albert Borgmann, who taught philosophy at the University of Montana and whom we mentioned in chapter 4. Borgmann contrasts "the device paradigm" we live in (and which few of us question) with what he prefers: "focal practices."[14] The key example here, as we saw earlier, is how we heat our homes. Before technology this was done by fire. But a fireplace was never just a source of heat. It was a hearth, which shares a root with the word "home." Pagan peoples put their gods by the hearth. All peoples told stories by it. They cooked food on it, passed on wisdom and practical skills (like how not to get burned, or sick from undercooked food!). It formed a way of life that included cutting wood, going to bed when the fire went out, and structuring routines of the household. That's a focal practice. A device paradigm gives us central heat. It pushes warm air into our home for a price by means we can't understand. No wisdom is gained, no toil extracted, no social pattern organized. Except every social pattern is organized. You *can't* refuse technology now: "To be against it is to choose confinement, misery, and poverty" (I mean, heat?!).[15] The very thing meant to bring us freedom has made us bound—to devices.

Borgmann suggests we engage in focal practices. You can count hamburgers served, he says, but you can't count the depth of meaning of a family meal. Cooking and talking and cleaning together. It's a pain—don't pretend otherwise. But it's what makes us human. Running is a focal practice. The pain and the joy of the activity are one. As long as it's not on a treadmill and instead plunges us into nature. Since Borgmann is from Montana, fly fishing is a focal practice for him. It requires skill, learned socially and with sweat; it makes dinner possible; and it's connected to nature, the original focal thing, and is largely untamed and untamable. A guitar is a focal thing. To learn it you have to be in a tradition with those who've played it before, and Guitar Hero is no substitute. I met Borgmann's daughter once. Naturally I had to ask how she grew up. No television, of course. And music lessons, always music lessons! Focal practices are "concrete, tangible, and deep, admitting of no functional equivalents; they have a tradition, structure, and rhythm of their own. They are unprocurable and finally beyond our control. They engage us in the fullness of capacities."[16] And here's the surprise: "They thrive in technological settings."[17] All the things I mentioned have a place for or even require technology. Running requires paths and shoes. Fly fishing requires poles and gear. The guitar requires an instrument. This is not Thoreau or the Unabomber (or lots of the theological critics of technology who type their books on computers and email them to agents). This leaves a limited circumscribed place for technology at the periphery of our lives. But it keeps trying to move back to the heart, like those pagan gods on the hearth or in our pockets.

Like most critics, Borgmann is most devastating when he simply holds up a mirror. Video technology, for example, is not "used by people as the crucial aid that finally allows them to develop into the historians, critics, musicians, sculptors, or athletes that they have always wanted to be. Rather, the main consequence of this technological development appears to be the spread of pornography."[18] Improved means to unimproved ends. . . .

Gay lists areas we Christians cannot allow to be taken over by technology—marriage, friendship, family, church, school, community organizations—a list that could continue nearly indefinitely.[19] Yet one must ask, How do those institutions communicate with their members these days? It is a Gnostic fantasy to try to escape from ordinary embodiment. Gay repeatedly bangs the table and yells "No!" (even in italics—look!): "*No!* Christians must stand—stubbornly, prophetically, and by reason of basic Christian conviction—squarely in the path of this fruitless exchange"—that is, for embodied goodness and against the "hyperreality of cyberspace."[20] Theologians of a certain sort like to imagine ourselves astride the path of progress, waving our hands and heroically yelling "Stop!" Barth and Bonhoeffer did it to the Nazis (sort of). Should we not now?

The church has always had some brave souls who stand up like that—"stubbornly, prophetically, and by reason of basic Christian conviction." These people are called monks and nuns. Historians cannot find the first monastic who left civilization for the desert in the ancient church. Saint Anthony is credited as the founder of monasticism, but he makes clear he learned the life from a predecessor. Scholars debate whether there were Jewish monastics before Jesus, like perhaps John the Baptist or the Essenes may have been. Suffice to say as long as there has been Christianity there have been women and men giving up money, sex, and power, vowing poverty, chastity, and obedience in the way of Jesus.

Sometimes they have banded together in communities called monasteries. Other times they have lived as hermits. Sometimes hermits live relatively near one another so they can celebrate the Eucharist together. Monastics are crucial, for they allow the rest of us to have a people to point to when someone objects, "Jesus can't mean that." For Jesus often says impossible things: that we must give up all our possessions, that we must forswear all violence, that we cannot even look at another person with lust, that we must rush to the back of the line and never elbow our way up to the seat of power. That can't be! We preachers are very good at providing asterisks to allow readers to think Jesus didn't actually mean it. But he did. And it's not impossible. Look—those monastics do these things. Sure, they're weird, and there aren't a lot of them. But there don't have to be a lot to show that the life is possible. If Jesus really did rise from the dead to inaugurate his kingdom, some of us need to be living a radical form of life as we await his return.

If Gay and other outright rejectors of technology are right, we need some people simply saying no. This means not just logging off Facebook for Lent or taking a Sabbath away from streaming but living a life so out of tune with our technologically mediated culture that the rest of the world stands up and takes notice.

Now be careful here—*actual* vowed religious in our day use digital technology in quite creative ways, as monastics have always done. They use websites to attract potential novices or to sell their products (Benedictine monasticism in Western Christianity has always insisted monastic houses have to support themselves financially). Monks often have cell phones and, presumably, social media. Today's monasticism may be a very different sort, then, though one fully dedicated to embodied relationship and to sacraments as the only sort of mediation. We need some Christians to vow to disassociate from the technology that ensnares the rest of us. Just a few who will show that the fullness of life is not on a phone. It is the face of another human being.

An anti-technological set of monastic vows won't be the answer for most of us. Vowed monasticism has never been the way of discipleship for most Christians. Yet we all need Christian community. Over against those in his church who were too confident that they could be Christian hermits, Saint Basil asked, "If you live alone, whose feet will you wash?"

David Kinnaman and Mark Matlock's research at Barna has documented some of the more alarming trends around young people's disillusionment with faith. But in a more recent book he studied the faith of "resilients"—that is, young people who stay in church.[21] What can we learn from these benevolent outliers? And lots of the answers revolve around their churches helping them navigate the "digital exile" we all now experience.

The primary form of entertainment for Gen Y and Z and younger is to stream videos on their phones. If the numbers are to be trusted, they spend hundreds of hours per year doing this. An hour a week of preaching at a church can do very little against this onslaught of flickering pixels. Algorithms *disciple* our young people. They turn to Google's search engine to find out how to ask someone out, what sex is about, what the meaning of life is. Why wouldn't they? It's much easier, and less embarrassing, than asking a flesh-and-blood human being. Young people are using "the screens in their pockets as their counselors, their entertainers, their instructors, and even their sex educators, among many other digital-Sherpa roles."[22] And not just young people.

What's the answer? Not just more individual discipline, though there has to be some of that. Not just a family that arranges its furniture and schedule and desires differently—though, as Crouch makes clear, that will help. We also need a church making an effort to help us all be different from the digital Babylon in which we dwell. The problem is that the church has often tried to appeal to young people by entertaining them, asking little from them, lowering the bar for discipleship so young people can hop over it with minimal effort—or be foisted over it against their will. The problem is that no one is fooled by church leaders as showmen or entrepreneurs. We often lose our brightest young people that way. Kinnaman and Matlock quote one teenager who was unimpressed by her youth pastor, saying he "was paid to be my friend."[23] Ouch.

What we need is to understand participation in church life as a demanding set of relationships. Those who are resilient in their faith are much more likely to have older friends who help disciple them as believers. And this discipleship does not only go one way—Kinnaman and Matlock insist on "reciprocal mentoring." Old and young together, not related to one another, meet to ponder Jesus and help one another follow him. Where else do meaningful relationships among people of different ages take place in our culture? The church is the rare place where it can even happen. Kinnaman and Matlock suggest older people show the scratch work on their discipleship. Where did they get it wrong? What have they learned the hard way? How do they advise their younger friends to live now? Sorting through the patterns this way is the beginning of wisdom. It allows the growing disciple to start to see the patterns for herself.[24]

The hallmark of the way we raise children now is striving for safety at all costs. We over-protect and leave our charges bored and rudderless, wrapped in cellophane, with their search engines as the only place left to ask brave questions. What if, instead, they (and all of us really) spent time with older Christians or younger ones who are the sort of people we are trying to become? With Jesus's beloved poor or with folks seriously committed to other faiths? The fruit born will not be narrowly Christian. Barna's research suggests that resilient disciples are *more* likely to inquire respectfully about the beliefs of their non-Christian neighbors than non-religious people are.[25] Kinnaman and Matlock insist that they and Barna are not anti-technology, just anti-foolishness. And it is foolishness to think a search engine can grow a disciple. An older disciple can. Or a younger one.

A friend closes his correspondence this way: "Don't take care. Take risks." It's a summons to discipleship.

The devices are upon us. There is no going back. Some should resist, on behalf of the rest of us. But all of us have to find the discipline to keep the devices in the role of mere tools, since they keep threatening to master all parts of our lives. And we cannot do this alone—it takes a church to help all of us be human and not merely screen presences. In most cases, the solution will not be a binary logic—either embodied or online. Used well, digital connections can lend to embodied ones. Apologies for returning to this, but we can't help it: 2 John, one of our briefest New Testament epistles, says this: "Although I have much to write to you, I would rather not use paper and ink; instead I hope to come to you and talk with you face to face, so that our joy may be complete" (2 John 12).[26] *In the Bible* the writer prefers to be with the church in person. But he cannot, so he writes this letter, *which becomes part of the Bible*. This epistle was a form of virtual communion. The writer and the church are "together" across distance in the form of a technologically enabled epistle (a wax tablet becomes a parchment, is delivered via mail on Roman roads and via boat, is read out to the group by a literate person, is preserved in a scroll, and then becomes a priceless manuscript). We are not anti-technology but anti-foolishness. Face-to-face presence is a good thing. But virtual presence is a good-enough second best that huge chunks of our Bible were originally just that. For while 2 John is short, Romans is not—and Paul wrote it to a church he had not yet met.

It has become a little lazy to say that church or theological education can only take place in person. I remember a colleague joking, "I refuse to teach my course, called 'incarnational theology,' online." Har. But as we have all learned too well during this recent pandemic, being online is also an embodied experience.[27] We have to sit there. Use our eyes. Concentrate. Take notes. Speak and listen. It's *differently* embodied, mediated by pixels and fiber and machines that non-specialists can't begin to understand or repair. But it is not exactly disembodied. It is even face-to-face. Those are others' faces we see on Zoom. We cannot touch or smell them. But neither is this communication disembodied or anonymous. It is often face-to-face. And it is often a good substitute.

God loves mediation. God reveals *through* things—creation, Israel, Jesus Christ, the church. Icons, sacraments, signs and wonders, glossolalia. When God's people try to see God face-to-face, things go poorly. We cannot see the living God and expect to live (Exod. 33:20). Yet God is constantly sharing God's self, usually in ways we do not expect—and usually in more humble ways than we might have imagined. Scripture promises that all these mediated glimpses of God will one day be replaced with face-to-face knowledge (Matt. 5:8; 1 Cor. 13:12). In the meantime, we do not try to avoid God's mediation. We luxuriate in it. As God seems to.

And we still should not commune online. It plays to our worst impulses as Protestants to reduce church to individual consumerism and Gnostic ideas in our heads or comfort in our hearts. The vast, cosmic gospel of God's new creation is reduced to me and Jesus and ideas that make me go to heaven and feel happy in the meantime. Resist it. But by all means, use the web for things it can be used for. Robert Jenson, whom we mentioned earlier, was the perfect stereotype of the curmudgeonly rejector of all things modern, and he had unsurprisingly disdainful things to say about virtual sacraments. But he suggested we use the web for things it can be used for, like doing theology, which is the very thing he, as a theologian, did for a living. We can speak true words of the living God in a way that teaches, encourages, and corrects, in a way that grows in friendship on the way to wisdom. We just shouldn't try to push water through that screen or bread or wine through those bytes. It is no bad thing to phone or text or email a spouse. But it is a better thing to be with them in person.

Recently, I (Andria) responded to a tweet asking for the most on-brand school memory that has affected how I am in the world today. Most of the memories that surfaced for people were those of getting in trouble, and mine was no exception. I recounted the time I was hauled into the principal's office of my Catholic elementary school and threatened with expulsion for participating in the Eucharist . . . *as an Anglican.*

At the age of eleven I had a strong desire to feast at the table. The Jesus I knew ate with Pharisees and prostitutes; certainly he would be willing to share his memory with a preacher's daughter who only missed one of her pre-confirmation classes. The theology of an open table is one that has shaped my own faith and also every conversation about online ministry I've had over the last five years. We cannot argue that we can be the church online if we can't eat together.

I will admit I am one of the "lower Protestants" Jason references in this chapter whose denomination appears to have reduced Communion to a consumerist comfort, but I argue with him regularly that he's wrong and that we haven't.

The first Communion meal the congregation I work for had after ceasing in-person worship in March 2020 was one of the most intentionally considered and celebrated meals I've been blessed with. Recognizing that the five hundred people gathered around the world in front of their screens on this particular Sunday were not all equipped with bread and juice, we did provide the pantry list so feared by my more orthodox friends. We didn't mention goldfish explicitly, but I wouldn't be surprised if the little cheddar crackers made someone's cut. And that would have been okay. We used the opportunity to look around us in the sanctuary and name the things that might further separate us from one another: The beautiful pottery chalice. The shared loaf. The chancel itself. To eat with one another we must all be given a place at the table, and so we made room. The Communion table was carried off the chancel and into the middle of the sanctuary. It was set with half a dozen different glasses and plates: some silver, some wicker, some pottery, some from IKEA. We placed on each rice crackers, juice boxes, wafers, wine, bread, water. And when it came time to bless the meal, we were invited into the corporate body of Christ through the Spirit and were asked to lift our hands so that all we had may be consecrated. We ate separately, from our pantries, and we remembered not only what it was like to be included but what it means to be whole.

As one local theologian responded to the service, when the temple was destroyed, God remained. Our open table was evermore extended.

Another theologian and minister on Canada's east coast, Andy O'Neill, is well versed in the conversation surrounding our denomination's ever-moving stance on virtual Communion. He reminds me over a video call in which I recounted this experience that we, the United Church of Canada, have made substitutions in this area before when we made the choice to support our siblings in recovery and not use wine. With each consideration the question around efficacy returns to the Scriptures. Is it imperative? Who are we to say God can't do a good thing here?

I know one thing for sure regarding the history of the United Church of Canada. Had the inaugural service on June 10, 1925, taken place one hundred, ninety, or even eighty years later, it would, without a doubt, have been broadcast live across the internet. The words of "The Old Hundredth"[28] would have been scrawled across the screen with invitation and jubilation for everyone to declare: *All people that on earth do dwell! Sing to the Lord with a cheerful voice!*

It is this reference to "all" that first drew me into the United Church of Canada and continues to govern my ministry. Here was a denomination of union, sacrament, doctrine, and evangelism that managed to proclaim an authentically liberal invitation to come, whoever you were, and feast at the table.

Belonging to a denomination that has, several times, re-worded the creeds to better encompass an ever-growing understanding of the complexities of being children of God in today's world has, perhaps, liberated us from the view that we simply *couldn't do it*. Nevertheless, the decision to have online Communion didn't happen overnight. It is still taking shape as we navigate the extent to which we'll be living like this and what a life post-pandemic might mean for those who choose to remain online. My prayer would be that we might save a seat for those for whom virtual Communion remains the only option now, or ever. O'Neill asks the question more boldly: "What love are we withholding if we put too many boundaries in place?"[29]

John Cassian, a contemporary of Augustine's and a monk's monk back in the fifth century, counsels a young, particularly food-focused abbot in his second conference. The young Germanus wonders how all the rules of the Christian faith can be applied at the same time. He struggles with the idea of fasting, pointing out that it is as sinful to break a fast as it is to decline hospitality in the form of sharing bread with a visiting brother. Cassian's counselor, an Archimandrite named Moses, replies that there is no escaping the Christian requirement of hospitality. "It would be quite ridiculous," he says, "to receive a brother at the table—or, rather, Christ himself—and then take nothing of the meal, to be there like a stranger."[30]

It is quite true that there is not a most righteous way to be together when we cannot be together, but Jesus knows that. From where I sit behind my screen on Sunday mornings, participating in a meal with some who are beside me and some who are far away, this remembrance is as close as we've ever been.

We might think of prayer generally, and the Eucharist specifically, as a sort of anti-technology. Not that they can be done without human action or ingenuity: bread and wine are products of human making, *homo faber* at work as God intends. Ancient teaching on baptism and medieval teaching on the Eucharist sound almost mechanical at points. Baptism works if done by a priest in apostolic succession with water in the name of the Holy Trinity. In the Eucharist, at the words of institution, the bread and wine change in their substance to be the body and blood of Christ, though their accidents—their outward appearance—remain unchanged. My (Jason's) Methodists agree that Christ is really present in the sacrament but shy away from any technical terminology about how. Every other church has its own eucharistic doctrines. These guidelines are the fruit of dogmatic dispute and clarification to help the church know the circumstances under which God promises to be present. Yet they are not conjuring tricks. We cannot summon the God of Israel against his will or to do our bidding. He is no genie in a bottle, no search-engine deity. Technology has what seems like an advantage but is not: you can tell if it "works." Sacraments have what seems like a disadvantage but is not: you cannot tell if it "works." You trust. As a community, you receive previous wisdom, practice it, and wait in hopeful expectation. There is a promise from a trustworthy God, but there is no tangible proof. Other than a people living as though the resurrection is real. It's not a light switch. There is nothing easy about it. It is life itself. In the flesh. Don't try it online.

• The obvious question: Can Christians celebrate Communion online? What about baptism? What of the other traditional sacraments, or sacrament-like, means of grace? Why or why not?

- All Christians would agree that Jesus has to have a body as real as ours, or we can't be saved. How might this physically incarnate God reach out to similarly incarnate people via digital means?

EIGHT

Daring to Speak for God

In a recent confab with other professionals around Vancouver, each person was asked what their organization's mission was. This question can set off memes of eyerolls from characters on *The Office*. Or it can be clarifying.

Why do we have preaching? What is it *for*? It might seem clear as day that preaching could be done online. But is it? The answer depends on what you think preaching is. The Lord Jesus is the first Christian preacher. And his bodily presence is, shall we say, contentious in the history of the church. Yet all Christians would agree there is no preaching without the presence of the risen One. And he has a penchant for appearing in places where we're sure he shouldn't and for vanishing when we wish he wouldn't.

One of the nonreligious professional people in the room that day works at a rape crisis center. She said her organization exists not only to stop sexual violence in her city and to heal its victims. That would be audacious enough, but it doesn't stop there. Its goal is to stop and heal sexual violence *everywhere*. As if that weren't enough already, she went further: "We want social justice everywhere." Some of us asked how realistic that goal was, however laudable. She replied, "I don't know. I just know how liberating our clients find it to see those words on our wall."[1]

Another works for a provincial government agency charged with worker safety. "Our goal is to keep all workers from injury or death." Like, forever?! "No, just on the job in our province. But why limit it? Aren't all workers in solidarity?"[2]

Similarly, our goal should be freedom from violence, not just for us but for all others. Such goals are so ambitious one could only imagine them arriving in some altogether-new world. Like the one Jesus brings.

What about preaching? Often enough, in mainline church settings, the goal seems to be commenting accurately on a little passage of Scripture. To be passingly not-boring enough to get through the morning. To be sure, above all, not to say anything racist/sexist/homophobic/anti-Jewish. To imagine one could hold one's head high if a seminary professor turned up. To harrumph about Trump and then take one's seat. If you're more liberally inclined, you want to make sure listeners feel vaguely guilty about some moral issue. If more conservative, you want to be sure they have the right ideas in their heads (your ideas, of course).

The ambition of our ostensibly secular neighbors shames us.

Perhaps this caricature of preaching is ungenerous. In theology it is often truer to say what God is not than what God is. By analogy, it is more reliable to say what preaching is not than what it is. It is not moralism—inflicting guilt for this or that. It is not commentary on world events—the *Times* can do that just fine on its own. It's not reading your exegetical notes. And please God, it's not entertainment. It's not even a call to conversion, though that's closer to the mark. It's not a summons to social justice, though again we're getting closer.

What if we described the purpose of preaching with similar ambition to those other two professionals? Our goal in preaching might be to announce that God, in Christ, is healing the entire cosmos. All those listening can take part in that healing work by the Spirit. That sort of preaching happens in church on Sundays over an open Bible for the gathered saints. But not only there. To watch Jesus preach, it also happens where people work, as fishers and farmers and Pharisees. It happens on the road, often accompanied by such signs and wonders as healing the sick. Preaching happens at the table and includes a rather awkward reordering of normal seating priorities and such unbearable intimacy as washing and anointing and kissing feet. It happens from his cross. And it happens in his resurrection. If it doesn't happen through us, it will happen some other way—even the stones will cry out (Luke 19:40). The Word is alive; it is near you, on your lips, and in your heart (Deut. 30:14). You can try to stop the proclamation of the Word, but it will only flash out farther, like a fire shut up in the bones (Jer. 20:9). God promises to do for all creation what he did for Jesus. Preaching simply announces that this resurrection and transfiguration of the cosmos is coming and, in fact, is already here.

Such preaching can even happen on the computer. You can say why it shouldn't, properly speaking, why there is this or that rule against it happening. But you'd run the risk of saying that God somehow *can't* work through such created means as digital technology. As though there were some portion of creation that does not belong to the God who made it all and is redeeming it all. Church authorities have done that sort of thing often. John Wesley remembered his own difficulty imagining preaching out of doors—"I would have thought the saving of a soul a sin if it did not happen in church," he mused later.[3] But "real" churches were no longer inviting him, and so he preached to those who would not come to church, in fields, at coal mines, to folks on their way to and from work. The pulpit from which he preached in those places is on display in a museum in North Carolina. That's right—he would roll a physical pulpit out into a field. He might have preached out of doors but not without a giant piece of furniture to stand on! God is much less discriminating than we are about the healing of creation. God just goes about repairing what we have ruined, announcing it through all the wrong people, through all kinds of unauthorized means.

Think, for a moment, about the resurrected Jesus preaching about himself from all the Scriptures. He meets two of his crestfallen disciples on the road. They are leaving Jerusalem, going back to their old lives before meeting him. Imagine the oceans of disappointment in their lament, "We had hoped he was the one to redeem Israel" (Luke 24:21). They have even heard about the resurrection (v. 24). But they did not understand the women's claim sufficiently even to disbelieve it—it just confused them. Crucified messiahs are, by definition, failed messiahs, crushed out, all the life gone. All the hopes about the redemption of Israel and the renewal of the world were, as it turns out, ill-founded. No ghost story or idle women's tales can undo those hard realities. Time to go back to a real job and to appropriately this-worldly and attainable hopes.

Then the risen Christ himself appears and walks with them. They don't recognize him—their "eyes were kept" from doing so (Luke 24:16). The unrecognized Christ proceeds to flirt with them. One of them asks, "Are you the only stranger in Jerusalem who does not know the things that have taken place there in these days?" (v. 18). Like a complete idiot, or like the one at the center of the things that have taken place, not only in Jerusalem but in every place since the world began, Jesus asks, "What things?" (v. 19). They tell the story, but they get it wrong.[4] They tell the story of Jesus *to* Jesus in a way that Jesus disapproves of: "Oh, how foolish you are" (v. 25).

I wonder how much of our preaching sounds that way in Jesus's ears?

Then Jesus proceeds to preach himself. Not in a synagogue—he's done that before, to not-altogether-happy results. Not in the temple. Not in any officially authorized religious building. And not "in" a church—no one has thought of a church as a building yet. Just on the road. To two disciples, not otherwise noteworthy folks, only one of whose names we know. "Beginning with Moses and all the prophets, he interpreted to them the things about himself in all the scriptures" (Luke 24:27). No New Testament to work with, he uses Israel's Scripture, which is all he needs.

Preaching doesn't end when the talking is done. A sermon never ends when the words stop. Not even with a sermon by the risen Christ to two of his original disciples. It leads to the table. He tries to walk on (Where you going, Jesus?! [Luke 24:28]). They urge him to stay. That's the response we aim for—that folks would yearn for more of Jesus's presence. At the table, he takes bread, blesses it, breaks it, and gives it to them. "Then their eyes were opened, and they recognized him; and he vanished from their sight" (v. 31). The two go and tell others, as one must do when the risen Christ gives of himself at the table to those who don't believe: "They told what had happened on the road, and how he had been made known to them . . ." In his resurrected presence with them? No. In the preaching? No. In their urging him to stay? No. ". . . In the breaking of the bread" (v. 35). Christian preaching is profoundly penultimate. It points ahead—to sharing a meal at table, to telling others about a crucified and risen Messiah, to the re-creation of the cosmos by Christ.

Notice the preached Word's tenuous relationship to Jesus's bodily presence. He is there with them but goes unrecognized even as he preaches "about himself" from the Scriptures (Luke 24:27). Then in the breaking of the bread their eyes are opened, they recognize him, and he vanishes (v. 31). The Christian tradition places enormous emphasis on the risen Christ's presence in the stranger, in the preached word, in the Eucharist. That is all appropriate. Yet just after he is present (unrecognized) in each in this story, he is absent (yet retroactively recognized) at its climax. The story promises its listeners that we can meet Jesus in the stranger, the story, the meal. But the moment we see him, he's gone. There is almost a negative corollary between recognition and presence in this story and so in the life of discipleship, following the risen Jesus. Christians have always seen Christ in the present and absent lover in the Song of Songs—it matches the ambiguous nature of his promised presence with us. Think of his own promises—he will never leave us. No, he will, but the Spirit will come. He'll be back. He's in the bread and wine, in the poor and in one another. But as soon as you think you see him, he's out. This is an unpredictable sort of body, to say the least. So the relationship between preaching and bodily presence is tenuous. At most we might say that the moment you are most sure of bodily presence, it is undone. He's gone ("and he vanished from their sight" [v. 31]).

Whatever else the coronavirus pandemic has done, it has recalibrated our sense of the relationship between bodily presence and preaching. We plotted this book partly as an attempt to overcome anxieties about doing ministry online. During the writing that goal changed. Recently the *only* ministry happening anywhere has been online. Yet the question of the book has remained the same: How do we use this potentially disembodied, Gnosticizing medium for fully embodied,

face-to-face discipleship? This is a harder question than a simple yes/
no can answer. Natalie Carnes of Baylor University speaks of our
other present controversy—the forceful removal of white supremacist monuments in North Atlantic countries.[5] Carnes has written on
iconoclasm and iconophilia in Christian tradition and today—so
what of it? Should the monuments come down (iconoclasm) or stay
(iconophilia)? Maybe neither. She suggests draping a mournful fabric
over the statues. That keeps us from forgetting a white supremacist
history or from celebrating it. It keeps a painful history before our
eyes as a means of mourning.

What would be a similarly creative answer beyond yes/no binaries
regarding digital life together?

Some reports during the pandemic have been of remarkable, almost miraculous church growth. One friend, Dan Matheson of the
Kitsilano site of Tenth Church here in Vancouver, preaches regularly
to 250 people on a Sunday. Some two thousand have been tuning in
to his sermons during quarantine. The internet can't say who those
people are though. Former members who've moved away? Folks randomly finding them on the web? He knows one thing for sure: preaching this way is more like the delivery of a television performance than
anything he's ever done in person. He is preaching without pastoring.
He can't see their faces, know how this or that line is landing in this or
that life. Yet there are other benefits. More voices can go into the production (the word choice is significant) of worship than ever before.
Scripture readers, people praying, and musicians can all vary more
easily than in in-person worship. Far more unpaid people are involved
than ever. He cites Andy Crouch, who suggests that our worship at
the moment will have to be global, with a maximum emphasis on
production value, and also local, with a maximum emphasis on the
relational at the granular level.[6] Previously, Dan has rarely spent time
on the phone calling folks on the rolls and asking how they are, if he
can pray with them. But he is now. Perhaps since Sunday is more of a
production than ever, he feels oilier asking for money. The pandemic
has made televangelists of us all.

Another preacher friend pastors in a left-leaning church in a ruby-
red state. His people protest US military adventures and pipeline
building, then worship Jesus on Sundays. They stay small, you won't

be surprised to learn—he rarely preaches to more than one hundred people. But during the pandemic he has seen more than one thousand logging in regularly. Again, who are they? Maybe a niche in a small town can go far deeper online than it ever could in person. But can those extra nine hundred people turn up for a march together? Not in person. Can they visit each other's front porches, share ideas and tea and friendship? Perhaps. This pastor knows one thing: he is drained all the time. Normally he gets reenergized on Sunday, worshiping together, getting ready for another week. Now his nerves are frayed over whether the technology will work. He never gets the hand-shaking, back-slapping recharge that he counts on. Instead he spends his days phoning and emailing and leading committee meetings. The screen says one thousand people are watching. That's . . . encouraging in a way and distressing in another. Who are they? What do we know about one another? Can we see any actual signs of discipleship pushing to the surface? The honest answer is, he dunno. But that doesn't mean they don't exist, does it?

Another friend is a Scripture scholar. He is in his first teaching position in a small town miles from anyone else who wants to study Scripture in Hebrew. The pandemic has brought an unexpected gift. Suddenly, he is now engaged in Torah study weekly with scholars from around the globe: Israel, Australia, America, Canada. They chew on the words, on the tenses, on the roots, on possible shades of meaning. Everyone on the call can keep up; no one needs remedial Hebrew help. The Torah study is a little like the kingdom come, Jews and Christians and others studying together, and it wouldn't have happened without technology.

Another pastor grants that this strange moment can foster new discoveries.[7] Innovation can always produce something fruitful. But the way the computer screen distances us can give folks another excuse to disengage from church. "It's not like they were lining up to get in before all this," he said. It is, indeed, a terrible question to have to ask oneself or one's family, "Where should we watch church this morning?" Church is that much further down the road to a consumable experience of entertainment, isolated from those without the same last name.

Then again, yet another friend is in a gritty, social justice–oriented ministry. His community is the go-to group for community organizing in their town. They're still doing that work, especially in an intense Black Lives Matter moment. It's all virtual at the minute, of course. And they find their work in their neighborhood all the more important. They take walks together and greet their neighbors on porches (with appropriate social distance, of course). People who don't normally want to talk with activists are suddenly hungry to talk to *anyone* and will engage. That's a start, a step on the way to the mutual recognition of Jesus's beloved community in the middle of an ordinary town.

Back here in BC we have been blessed with extraordinary leadership during the pandemic. Dr. Bonnie Henry, the province's chief health officer, has become something of a folk hero, with her face emblazoned on T-shirts, a designer shoe and a craft beer named for her. She gives out her health information with wisdom and authority but also with kindness and consideration. Her tagline is "be kind, be calm, be safe," and when she says it, we all nod, *Okay, that's a good idea.* Canadians believe in "peace, order, and good government," as opposed to Americans' "life, liberty, and the pursuit of happiness." We're the Brits who didn't revolt, after all. We tend to be more of a rule-following bunch, less inclined to define freedom as the right to infect or shoot our neighbors. But there is another story to the health of this province. BC is famously home to enormous expat communities from Asia, India, Iran, and elsewhere. Prognostications suggested we would get clobbered by the virus for that very reason—folks traveling back and forth. What actually happened is that those expat communities heard from home how bad the virus was. Some of them are readier to wear masks already than white Canadians are. So they started masking, staying home, isolating and quarantining before the rest of their neighbors did. When leadership wanted to open back up, they often heard from those communities a simple no thanks. There have been disgusting instances of violent racism against members of these communities for allegedly bringing the virus to Canada (the strain among us actually came from Europe, but never mind). But as it turns out, our immigrants are a hedge against illness, a strength in the body politic, a source of life and health. The God of Pentecost must be pleased.

Preachers announce the reign of Christ. And part of that announcement is *pointing it out where no church planned it*. God's new creation is presently breaking out everywhere. It is by no means limited to churchly programming or planning. It is intended for the benefit of the whole world, for the healing of the nations, for the remaking of the universe. Christian preaching heralds its arrival wherever it can be seen. Look! There it is, breaking forth, do you not perceive it? God is always making a new thing, streams in the desert, a way in the wilderness.

Christian preaching announces that, despite all evidence to the contrary, a slain Lamb rules everything that is (Rev. 5:5–6). This can be hard to see in the best of times, let alone the worst. Yet it remains true. We invite our hearers, and ourselves really, to realign our lives in accordance with that coming and already-present reign. Christ is risen. He is raising all things. You'll see. One day everyone will see.

What's that, you say? You can't do that on the internet? The right response might be the sort of incredulity of those who are challenged on whether you can baptize babies or ordain women or gay people. Do I believe in those things? Hell, I've seen 'em! There are good reasons for nervousness about preaching online, no doubt. There are also dangers about preaching IRL, which we have perhaps not pondered enough. Preachers risk standing up in front of everybody and claiming to speak for God. We have done real harm in this, as any critic of religion will tell you, and not a few of its loyal daughters and sons. The response is not to forswear such pretense. It is to speak *well* for God. Beautifully. Graciously. Truly. Christ is risen and reigning over all things, even the digital world in all its strange depths. If we remain silent, the stones will cry out. If we point him out and others see him, really see him, he'll vanish. If we don't see him, he'll be there anyway, teaching about himself from Scripture and all creation. So go ahead and point him out, hail and herald him, risen and raising. Even here. Especially here.

- Where have you seen the rule of the slain Lamb in a surprising place—perhaps even where you think it "shouldn't" be?

- Is online preaching making available some set of gifts that preaching IRL seems not to? What do we lose preaching this way that can't be found again?

Conclusion

No Unmediated God

It may seem like a new question when we ponder the relationship between Christian faith and media. Christian faith is old, ancient, dating back to Abraham or even to Adam. Media is new, dating back not further than the invention of the television, telephone, or telegraph. There are no such tele's in the Bible. The question is how to relate this old, stodgy, ancient faith with the new, technologically advancing, up-to-the-nanosecond digital world.

But that would be incorrect.

Christianity is an inherently mediated faith. All it is, is media. There is no direct access to the God of Israel, fleshed in Jesus Christ. You can only approach this God mediated through material means. God appears in a burning bush. In a whirlwind on a mountain. In a cloud by day and a pillar of fire by night. You can try to see the God of Israel face-to-face. Moses asked for that privilege himself, on Mount Sinai, amid his reception of God's law. "You can't," God said. "You'll die. But we can put you in the cleft of the rock, I'll pass by, and you can see my backside" (see Exod. 33:18–23). That's all we get when we ask to see God face-to-face: a glimpse of God's butt. I'm paraphrasing. But only a little.

You think that's weird? Things get even weirder in the New Testament. Jesus, after a remarkable ministry of teaching and healing and miracling and exorcizing demons, gathers with his disciples for a last meal in an upper room. In some of the versions of the story this is a Passover meal; in others that is not obvious. What *is* obvious is that this is unlike any other meal they, or we, have ever had. He takes bread, blesses it, breaks it, and gives it to each of them, saying, "Take, eat, this is my body, given for you, do this in remembrance of me." When supper is ended he takes the cup, again blesses it, and gives it to each of them, and says, "This is my blood of the covenant, poured out for you and for many for the forgiveness of sins, do this as often as you drink it in remembrance of me" (see Matt. 26:26–28; Luke 22:19–20). As a minister who presides over the sacrament, I can't even type those words without intoning them liturgically in my mind. The whole history of Christian theology, with all its glories and all its sordidness, can be told as a commentary on this passage. Most of that can be boiled down to the question of whether Christ's promised presence in the sacrament is real (answer: yes!) or metaphorical (answer: yes!). For our purposes, we just note how profoundly *mediated* it is. Jesus Christ promises ongoing access to himself in a meal, in bread and in wine. No meal, no Jesus. As he says in one place, "Unless you eat the flesh of the Son of Man and drink his blood, you have no life in you" (John 6:53). Many of his disciples then leave—who can handle such a bodily, tactile, cannibalistic-sounding faith?! But take that meal, and you get all the Jesus you can handle and more. Saint Augustine says most meals have us eat food and digest it so it becomes part of our bodies. But in the Lord's Supper, we eat, *and it digests us*, making us into the body of Christ.

This is the original medium: a bite of bread, a sip of wine. Marshall McLuhan famously declared, as part of his criticism of modern media, that "the medium *is* the message."[1] Most subsequent commentators have suggested that he overstates. Content does matter. There is a difference between, say, a documentary on Mother Teresa and a Stallone/Gibson/Arnie carnage movie on television. But he would have been right had he been talking about the sacrament. Jesus enters into a world of broken relationships with a meal of repair. At his Last Supper, he was preparing his disciples for his passion, when his body would be torn apart, his blood spilt, his divine personhood joined to all those others torn apart, poured out, discarded. But his torn-apart and emptied body would then be filled with resurrection life. When we gather for worship, we too are filled with resurrection life—a life we offer and witness to the world. What is now scattered, torn, emptied, God is working to gather, repair, fill. But not without this bread, this wine, this body, and all other bodies as well.

Another mediation is via water. It conducts more than electricity. It conducts grace. It even predates Jesus. The first thing he does in his ministry is submit to the baptism of John. At first this was a Jewish cleansing ritual, a sign of being born into the age to come. But when Jesus went under the water, it became something more: birth into the Christian church, which is its own sort of entry into the age to come. Jesus, Origen said, is the kingdom in person.[2] Jesus was baptized by John, but he baptizes us into his own body. There is no entry into the Christian life without baptism by water and the Spirit. It signifies our washing with grace, our new life in the womb of the church, and the dousing of the Holy Spirit. Some Christians have tried to speak of entry into Jesus's people without the water: Quakers and the Salvation Army try to experience the spiritual grace of sacraments without the physical means; Pentecostals emphasize a baptism of the Holy Spirit separate from the sacrament with water, and the wider church has agreed that for unbaptized martyrs, their blood is baptism enough. But the wider church has generally maintained that you need the physical water for the thing to *work*. These creative minority traditions stand out for their seriousness. The rest of us try to lower the bar as far as we can. All you need to enter the Christian life is water and the name of God, the Holy Trinity. With those two elements, you're in. Without the medium of water, you're not.

This water is not solitary. After baptism, all water reminds us of the womb in which we are nurtured in faith. The rain outside my window now (this *is* British Columbia!) is a reminder of baptism. When friends in South Sudan see rain, they exclaim, "God is blessing us!" Saint Francis is often quoted as saying that when it rains, we should remember our baptism. Now that God has touched water, all water speaks of grace, conducts mercy to us and through us to others. Our bodies are mostly water. The earth's surface is mostly water. There is no lack of media, just as there is no lack of grace. Memory of baptism also includes those who baptized us. And those who baptized them. And those who baptized them. All the way back to the apostles. Christian faith is endlessly mediated. It has finger-prints all over it. And these, unlike our sins, can never be washed off.

The authors of this book belong to Protestant, Reformed tradi-tions in which the two sacraments are baptism and the Lord's Sup-per alone—those clearly commanded by the Lord Jesus and (nearly) universally agreed upon among Christians. But our Catholic siblings may be more right than Protestants are as they stretch the sacrament list to include confession, marriage, the anointing of the sick, confir-mation, and ordination. Each of these claims an origin in Jesus's own ministry (though Jesus's mere presence at the wedding at Cana is a *little* tenuous). But each does extend Jesus's ministry of repairing the world. Confession assures the penitent of Christ's grace. Marriage sees the spouse as the very presence of Christ. Anointing continues Jesus's ministry of healing the world. Confirmation allows the one baptized to accept the grace with which Christ has accepted her. And ordination shows that God is good enough to us to set aside some in the community to lead the rest of us to new life. Each of these is a mediation. Confession requires a priest and gestures and words of consolation. Marriage requires another person and mutual delight. Anointing requires oil and prayers for healing. Confirmation and ordination require the laying on of hands. These are reiterations of Jesus's ministry in the world—and they are radically joined to the physical gesture. Theologians and canon lawyers may debate whether the sacraments are valid if one or more element is missing (not a few ministers can attest they have had to baptize without water or anoint without oil—we are forgetful creatures!). But that division between Protestants' two and Catholics' seven sacraments may be entirely too narrow. The church fathers and mothers speak of dozens of sacra-ments, including things like the reading of Scripture, the "salting" of a catechumen before training for baptism, the relics or bones of saints, the veneration of icons, and many more.

Ours is an embodied faith, and so grace always comes through material, mediated means. No media, no grace. Christ has promised, and bound himself, to be savingly present in baptism and Eucharist, in marriage, ordination, confirmation, confession, and anointing, but God is *able* to be present in any medium in all of creation. As this is sometimes put, God has bound us to the sacraments, but God has not bound God's self.[3] God *can* be present in anything. There would be no thing at all without God's providence. But God "has" to be present in the sacraments. God has promised nothing less.

During spring 2020 amid protests of police brutality in North America, some looting broke out. A Catholic bookstore was looted on Michigan Avenue in Chicago, with appropriate lamenting on social media. But then one interrogator asked the sister managing the store a question that may sound odd to Protestant ears: Was the blessed sacrament disturbed? The store has a chapel in the back. Catholic priests consecrate the host and leave it for adoration by the faithful. The sister assured the questioner that looters' sacramental theology is apparently not overly developed. The sacrament, more valuable than petty cash or intact windows, was untouched.

To put the point in more Protestant-friendly terms: consider the persons through whom you learned Christian faith. For disproportionate numbers of us, this was a grandparent. For others, perhaps a college friend presented the gospel in a way that invited us to accept Jesus's lordship and follow as disciples. For others it might be a celebrated evangelist through whom they learned the companionship of Jesus. We cannot now think of the gospel without its mediation through these friends—and these are only the ones we know about! There are countless others going back through time and extending around the globe to whom we are connected in the one body of Christ. There is no gospel without all of these. Cut us off from these others and we die. Connected to the body we bear fruit, with life pulsing through the whole body, to and through us and others.

The God of the Bible loves mediation. This God only appears *through*, never solo—only *with*, never unaccompanied. God chooses and marries and refuses to part from *a people*. God then doubles down on that choice by choosing to be born of a woman from that people. Scholars call it the scandal of particularity: this God has an address. God *lives* at One Temple Way in Jerusalem.[4] The God who cannot be contained settles down in a locale. Western individualism always wants to reduce things to the "I," the me, the solo, that's what individualism is. God is always working to expand to the corporate, the we, the embodied, the mutual. That's who God is. Enlightenment and modern critiques of the particularity of God presume that God should work universally, all at once, on everybody—anything less would be unfair, narrow. God actually agrees. But God's *way* of saving everyone, every particle of the creation God made in the first place, is to start with the specific—Israel and the church. God's work is shaped like a womb. He is born of Mary to renew the entire cosmos. When Saint Augustine sees references to the first person in the Psalms, the "I," he says that must be Jesus speaking. No one else could be that expansive a speaker, that inclusive a praiser. And of course Jesus is God not only in himself but in a way that includes all others. He is God *head and members*, as Paul often says (1 Cor. 12:27). As the head of the body, he is Jesus of Nazareth, Messiah of Israel and Savior of the world. He joins each of us as the members of the body, as constituent parts. Not just the good ones (for Augustine there *are* no good ones!). But the lousy members, the undeserving, the ones "we" would exclude. God is scandalously inclusive. That's what it means to be the God of Israel and of Jesus.

Think with me (Jason) here of the practice of pilgrimage. Christians, like others, have said we must occasionally get up and go to find God (Gen. 12:1). It's not just that the destination is holy, though it is—no objection to Lourdes, Santiago, or the holy place in walking distance from where you read. God seems so generous in sharing holiness with creation that it's almost wasteful, thoughtless by our lights. The destination is holy, but so is every step. We must leave where we are comfortable, recognized, familiar, and go where we are none of those things. Where we have to trust for each meal and each time of rest. Where we are needy and dependent on strangers. To borrow from our religious cousin, Malcolm X realized the potential goodness of white Muslims while pilgrimaging alongside them to Mecca. A friend of mine realized the blessedness of the poor while on a mission trip in Appalachia, hearing of economic and family desolation and then "hugging it out with sweaty strangers."[5] We realize God has almost capriciously left holiness everywhere, deposited it for anyone to find—maybe even back in our "ordinary" lives, where we can't normally see it. God binds us to people we would not have chosen, makes us care about places we would not care about on our own, unites us in an intimacy not otherwise on our itinerary. Willie

Jennings points out that when Peter is accosted by Jerusalem church leaders for going to the gentiles with the gospel, he does not say he realized the error of his previous ways, or that all people are equal. He says, effectively, "I didn't want to go! God made me."[6] Like Israel in the wilderness, like the church going out two by two with no provisions, God asks for a risky departure that includes a new joining with previously undesired people. Because that's where we find God.

God is endlessly, almost recklessly, mediated. And that is the God on whom we must reflect in a digital age. We have these tools. They can lead to disembodied, atomized, other-free life. No icon of this is more obvious than the solo person on the phone ignoring others in the room to whom they may be married, befriended, or, most promising on the Bible's reckoning, a stranger. The devices hollow out lives on our own. But faith expands them. Faith binds us not only to those with our last name but to those our race or culture tells us to despise. It says, "Go—I will meet you there, and only there." We must use these potentially disembodying and Gnostic media to trip ourselves and others into a radically embodied, other-inclusive faith and life. We have to be a stumbling block to hurl ourselves and others into an aggressively incarnational way of living. The devices will not do that by themselves. *We* will not do that by ourselves. We are sinners, aggressively turned in on ourselves, obsessed with ourselves and what makes our lives better. That's not the fault of the devices. It's the fault of the fall. God in Christ by the Spirit is working to turn us inside out, from ourselves to others (especially the troubling others!), so we would empty ourselves for the "undeserving." That's who God is, and in the gospel it is who God invites humanity to be.

- What is the most surprising means by which God has mediated grace to you? To your community?
- Why do we go on seeking an unmediated reflection of God, when God seems to prefer indirect presence?
- What do we do with passages that seem to suggest a more immediate presence of God (e.g., Exod. 24:9–18)?

Notes

Introduction The End Is Near

1. Quoted in Daniel Walker Howe, *What Hath God Wrought? The Transformation of America, 1815–1848* (New York: Oxford University Press, 2007), 3. This quotation originally appeared in "The Magnetic Telegraph," *Ladies' Repository* 10 (1850), 61–62.

2. Henry David Thoreau, "Walden," in *The Portable Thoreau*, ed. Jeffrey S. Cramer (New York: Penguin Classics, 2012), 239.

3. *The Personal Memoirs of U.S. Grant*, vol. 1 (New York: Charles L. Webster, 1885), 11.

4. Wendell Berry, *Jayber Crow* (Washington, DC: Counterpoint, 2000), 281–82.

5. Thoreau, "Walden," 239.

6. This is part of the extensive Carlyle Marney lore among preachers in the US South. See, for example, his book *Carpenter's Son* (Wake Forest, NC: Chanticleer, 1984).

7. Sherry Turkle, *Alone Together: Why We Expect More from Technology and Less from Each Other* (New York: Basic Books, 2011).

8. Phil Vinter, "Zadie Smith Pays Tribute to Computer Software That Blocks Internet Sites Allowing Her to Write New Book without Distraction," *Dailymail.com*, September 1, 2012, https://www.dailymail.co.uk/news/article-2196718/Zadie-Smith-pays-tribute-software-BLOCKS-internet-sites-allowing-write-new-book-distractions.html. It may be that headline writing is a lost art that is never coming back.

9. See Ben Quash and Michael Ward, eds., *Heresies and How to Avoid Them: Why It Matters What Christians Believe* (Grand Rapids: Baker Academic, 2007).

10. It's a common sentiment, but one example is David Kelsey, "Spiritual Machines, Personal Bodies, and God: Theological Education and Theological Anthropology," in *Teaching Theology and Religion* 5, no. 1 (January 2003). An excellent riposte to this way of putting things is Deanna Thompson's *The Virtual Body of Christ in a Suffering World* (Nashville: Abingdon, 2016). Thompson's own experience of suffering showed her that others could be the body of Christ to her, from afar, when her hospital room in the cancer ward was physically inaccessible. Many more have had similar experiences during the worldwide pandemic of 2020–21.

11. I heard this not on the internet but from a friend who was there, so it must be true.

12. Sven Birkerts, *The Gutenberg Elegies: The Fate of Reading in an Electronic Age*, 2nd ed. (New York: Faber & Faber, 2006), 229. Birkerts wrote that as the closing words to his 1994 book. The 2006 second edition includes his revised thoughts after parenthood.

13. This is one of the themes of Marty's massive project on fundamentalism, but you can hear it in his own voice here: https://berkleycenter.georgetown.edu/posts/martin-marty-on-the-fundamentalism-project.

14. Rowan Williams, *Why Study the Past? The Quest for the Historical Church* (Grand Rapids: Eerdmans, 2005), 52.

15. Nicholas Carr, *The Shallows: What the Internet Is Doing to Our Brains*, 2nd ed. (New York: Norton, 2020).

Chapter 1 Putting on the New Self

1. Peter Rollins, "Atheism for Lent," https://peterrollins.com.

2. As recounted in Peter Rollins's *The Idolatry of God: Breaking Our Addiction to Certainty and Satisfaction* (New York: Simon & Schuster, 2012), 55.

3. Mark Hall, "Facebook," Encyclopedia Britannica, May 29, 2019, https://www.britannica.com/topic/facebook.

4. The description comes from Peter Short, former moderator of the United Church of Canada. This is a common refrain from the writer and speaker, one that the I (Andria) wrote down in pages of notes from a workshop titled "Sowing Promise, Growing Leaders," in October 2019 in Osoyoos, British Columbia.

5. William Harmless, *Augustine & the Catechumenate* (Minneapolis: Liturgical Press, 1995), 314.

6. Philip K. Dick, *Do Androids Dream of Electric Sheep?* (New York: Ballantine, 1968), 8.

7. Eric Stoddard, "Digital Privacy: A Squandered Gift," *Modern Believing* 52, no. 4 (October 2011): 27, https://doi.org/10.3828/MB.52.4.23.

8. Richard A. Oppel and Kim Barker, "New Transcripts Detail Last Moments for George Floyd," *New York Times*, July 8, 2020, https://www.nytimes.com/2020/07/08/us/george-floyd-body-camera-transcripts.html.

9. Henri Nouwen, *Life of the Beloved: Spiritual Living in a Secular World* (New York: Crossroad, 1992), 32–33.

10. The author of this chapter is usually the one making this joke, but similar sentiments can be gleaned from the research of Lee Rainie, Sara Kiesler, Ruogu Kang, and Mary Madden, "Anonymity, Privacy and Security Online," Pew Research Center, September 5, 2013, https://www.pewresearch.org/internet/2013/09/05/anonymity-privacy-and-security-online.

11. Dietrich Bonhoeffer, *Life Together: The Classic Exploration of Christian Community* (New York: HarperOne, 2009), 112–13. As explored also in the thesis of Nicola J. Wilkes, "Private Confession of Sin in the Theology of Dietrich Bonhoeffer" (PhD diss., University of Cambridge, 2015).

12. "Digital Literacy in the Classroom. How Important Is It?," *Resource Ed: A Promethean Blog*, accessed May 2020, https://resourced.prometheanworld.com/digital-literacy-classroom-important.

13. Rana el Kaliouby, *Girl Decoded: A Scientist's Quest to Reclaim Our Humanity by Bringing Emotional Intelligence to Technology* (New York: Currency, 2020), 6.

14. I took this invitation to read Tillich in a technological light from several conversations with theologian and United Church of Canada minister colleague of mine Andy O'Neill.

15. Paul Tillich, *Systematic Theology*, vol. 3, *Life and the Spirit: History and the Kingdom of God* (Chicago: University of Chicago Press, 1963), 152, 139.

16. Rowan Williams, *Lost Icons: Reflections on Cultural Bereavement* (Edinburgh: T&T Clark, 2000), 166.

17. Shannon Dingle (@ShannonDingle), "Yep. Lots of my prayers this year have been 'WTF God???,'" Twitter, July 23, 2020, 8:19 p.m., https://twitter.com/ShannonDingle /status/1286455857853734912.

18. Max Roser, Hannah Ritchie, and Esteban Ortiz-Ospina, "Internet," Our World in Data, https://ourworldindata.org/internet. Roser, Ritchie, and Ortiz-Ospina explore the numerics of people using the internet globally. Examples of these particular questions being asked in online communities can be found all over social media, a recent example being the prompt of Kate Bowler on Twitter and Instagram inviting people to "share the simple things we love to hear to get through the pain." Kate Bowler (@KatecBowler), "Since the self-help industry is a lie but we need real encouragement right now," Twitter, July 22, 2020, 10:46 a.m., https://twitter.com/katecbowler/status/1285949233208729600.

19. See "Social Media, Social Life: Teens Reveal Their Experiences," Common Sense Media, 2018, https://www.commonsensemedia.org/sites/default/files/uploads/research /2018_cs_socialmediasociallife_fullreport-final-release_2_lowres.pdf; and Aaron Smith, "Why Americans Use Social Media," Pew Research Center, November 15, 2011, https:// www.pewresearch.org/internet/2011/11/15/why-americans-use-social-media.

20. Kaliouby, *Girl Decoded*, 5.

21. Jason Byassee, "Rachel Held Evans, Public Theologian," *Christian Century*, August 27, 2019, https://www.christiancentury.org/article/critical-essay/rachel-held-evans -public-theologian.

22. Substantial research affirms these experiences of social media, but for recent and engaging explorations, see Andrew Perrin, "Americans Are Changing Their Relationship with Facebook," Pew Research Center, September 5, 2018, https://www.pewresearch.org/fact-tank /2018/09/05/americans-are-changing-their-relationship-with-facebook; Elizabeth Dwoskin, "Quitting Instagram: She's One of the Millions Disillusioned with Social Media. But She Also Helped Create It," *Washington Post*, November 13, 2018, https://www.washington post.com/technology/2018/11/14/quitting-instagram-shes-one-millions-disillusioned-with -social-media-she-also-helped-create-it; Cal Newport, "Why You Should Quit Social Media," filmed June 2016 in Tysons, Virginia, TEDx video, 13:50, https://www.ted.com /talks/cal_newport_why_you_should_quit_social_media?language=en; Andrew Sullivan, "I Used to Be a Human Being," *New York Magazine*, September 19, 2016, https://nymag .com/intelligencer/2016/09/andrew-sullivan-my-distraction-sickness-and-yours.html.

23. Cal Newport, *Digital Minimalism: Choosing a Focused Life in a Noisy World* (New York: Penguin, 2019), 61.

24. Tristan Harris, "How Better Tech Could Protect Us from Distraction," filmed December 2014 in Brussels, Belgium, TEDx video, 14:48, https://www.ted.com/talks/tristan _harris_how_better_tech_could_protect_us_from_distraction?language=en.

25. Emily Dean Hund, "The Influencer Industry: Constructing and Commodifying Authenticity on Social Media" (PhD diss., University of Pennsylvania, 2019), https://reposi tory.upenn.edu/edissertations/3636, 144–49.

Chapter 2 A Pastoral Personality

1. Deborah Linton, "'I Have More Followers than the C of E': Meet the Religious Stars of Instagram," *The Guardian*, June 20, 2020, https://www.theguardian.com/world/2020 /jun/20/more-followers-than-c-of-e-religious-stars-of-instagram.

2. This photo appeared on Brereton's Twitter in August 2020 (https://twitter.com /RevDaniel). Brereton habitually deletes tweets, so this post is no longer visible.

3. Responses from Brereton come from an email correspondence with me (Andria) on July 21, 2020.

4. Daniel Brereton, email correspondence with Andria, July 21, 2020.

5. The quotations from Kast come from a Zoom interview conducted August 25, 2020.

6. Jim Keat, Zoom interview, July 22, 2020.

7. A business strategy of Vaynerchuk's from the beginning, he'll often say things to the effect of "Twitter is not about how to get more followers! Get in there and have a conversation!" Gary Vaynerchuk, "How to Use Twitter Like an Expert," garyvaynerchuk.com, 2013, https://www.garyvaynerchuk.com/infographic-how-to-use-twitter-like-an-expert.

8. Thomas Irby, FaceTime interview, March 20, 2020.

9. Craig Sailor and Kate Martin, "Spanish Flu Put Tacoma into a Panic and Sent Its Young Men and Women to Early Graves," *News Tribune*, May 25, 2018, https://www .thenewstribune.com/news/local/article210234789.html.

10. H. Richard Niebuhr, "The Emerging New Conception of the Ministry," in H. Richard Niebuhr, *The Purpose of the Church and Its Ministry* (New York: Harper & Brothers, 1956), accessed online at Religion-Online.org, http://media.sabda.org/alkitab-2/Religion -Online.org%20Books/Niebuhr%2C%20H.R%2C%20Williams%2C%20D.%20D.%20 %26%20Gustafson%2C%20J.M.%20-%20The%20Purpos.pdf, 35–40.

11. Thomas Irby, email correspondence with Andria, July 18, 2020.

12. The quotations from Kast come from a Zoom interview conducted August 25, 2020.

13. Thomas à Kempis, *The Imitation of Christ*, trans. Leo Sherley-Price (London: Penguin, 1952), 29.

Chapter 3 The Opposite of Technology

1. I take this point from Brandon O'Brien, *The Strategically Small Church* (Bloomington, MN: Bethany, 2010).

2. Albert Borgmann, *Technology and the Character of Contemporary Life: A Philosophical Inquiry* (Chicago: University of Chicago Press, 1984), 40–47. See also Wendell Berry's essay "Why I Am Not Going to Buy a Computer," in *What Are People For?* (New York: North Point, 1990), 170–77.

3. My friend John Varden points out that we are always a little residually impressed with technology when we remember life before it. My parents were like this with air conditioning, and my grandparents with indoor plumbing and refrigerators.

4. Quentin J. Schultze, *Habits of the High-Tech Heart: Living Virtuously in the Information Age* (Grand Rapids: Baker Academic, 2002), 13.

5. Schultze, *Habits of the High-Tech Heart*, 22.

6. See David Kelsey, "Spiritual Machines, Personal Bodies, and God: Theological Education and Theological Anthropology," in *Teaching Theology and Religion* 5, no. 1 (January 2003), 6. This article is a précis of what became the much larger book project.

7. Kelsey, "Spiritual Machines, Personal Bodies," 6–7.

8. Kelsey, "Spiritual Machines, Personal Bodies," 8.

9. Kelsey, "Spiritual Machines, Personal Bodies," 9.

10. Mitchell Landsberg, "'Theology after Google' Conference Takes Look at Religion in the Web Era," *Los Angeles Times*, March 15, 2010: https://www.latimes.com/archives /la-xpm-2010-mar-15-la-me-beliefs15-2010mar15-story.html.

11. Landsberg, "'Theology after Google' Conference."

12. Jeff Jarvis, *What Would Google Do?* (San Francisco: HarperBusiness, 2011), 11.

13. Jeff Jarvis, "Media Owners: Ask Not What Facebook Can Do for You . . . ," *The Guardian*, June 11, 2007, https://www.theguardian.com/media/2007/jun/11/mondaymedia section.news.

14. John Palfrey and Urs Gasser, *Born Digital: Understanding the First Generation of Digital Natives* (New York: Basic Books, 2008), 135.

15. Bobby Chernov, "How Many Blogs Are Published Per Day in 2020?," techjury, January 4, 2021, https://techjury.net/blog/blogs-published-per-day/#gref.

16. Palfrey and Gasser, *Born Digital*, 185.

17. I take the description "underdetermined" from Stephen F. Fowl, *Engaging Scripture* (Oxford: Blackwell, 1998). He contrasts modernist confidence that biblical criticism can serve up *the* meaning of a text (a determinate approach) with postmodern suspicion of singular meaning (anti-determinate). He proposes instead an "underdetermined" hermeneutic: he is going to offer the best reading of a text possible, without pretending he has landed on the single "meaning" the biblical author had in mind, without the playful despair of resisting meaning altogether. Meaning is a function of what communities do with texts, not a property lodged in texts themselves that is waiting to be dislodged by proper technique.

18. Larry Hurtado speaks of the "bookishness" of the ancient church, which produced a surprising amount of letters and manuscripts and treatises compared with its neighbors. See Larry Hurtado, *Destroyer of the Gods: Early Christian Distinctiveness in the Roman World* (Waco: Baylor University Press, 2017), 105–41.

19. The reference to 2 John comes from John Dyer, *From the Garden to the City: The Redeeming and Corrupting Power of Technology* (Grand Rapids: Kregel, 2011).

20. Rowan Williams, *Why Study the Past? The Quest for the Historical Church* (Grand Rapids: Eerdmans, 2005), 52.

21. See especially chapters 5 and 9 of Graham Ward's *Cities of God* (New York: Routledge, 2000).

22. Charles Taylor, *A Secular Age* (Cambridge, MA: Belknap, 2007), 37–42.

23. See Robert Jenson, "The Church and Mass Electronic Media," in *Essays in Theology of Culture* (Grand Rapids: Eerdmans, 2005), 156–62. This work is a masterful (and underread) collection.

24. His actual words: "I don't know if it's right to say that we're not forming institutions. How do we know? They may be there more than we know. What people are doing through communication could be a very early development of certain kinds of institutions today." "Stanley Hauerwas: What Only the Whole Church Can Do," Faith & Leadership, December 21, 2009, https://faithandleadership.com/multimedia/stanley-hauerwas-what -only-the-whole-church-can-do.

25. I take the description from Monica Coleman's profile of pastor Tony Lee in "Go-Go Preaching: New Media at Community of Hope AME Church," Kinetics Live, December 14, 2011, http://kineticslive.com/2011/12/14/go-go-preaching-new-media-at-community -of-hope-ame-church.

26. Trisha Ping, "Bill McKibben Looks into the Future of Our Changed Planet," BookPage, March 29, 2011, https://bookpage.com/interviews/8571-bill-mckibben-lifestyles#.X9K-ws1Kg2w.

27. Richard Rodriguez, "Final Edition: Twilight of the American Newspaper," *Harper's Magazine*, November 2009, https://harpers.org/archive/2009/11/final-edition.

28. I take this way of telling the story of the parable of the sower from my mentor James Howell—of Myers Park United Methodist Church in Charlotte, NC—who often uses it in stories and sermons and blog posts.

Chapter 4 Jesus's Own Family

1. This is one of Stanley Hauerwas's oft-repeated aphorisms, worked out in essays like "The Radical Hope in the Annunciation: Why Both Single and Married Christians Welcome Children," in *The Hauerwas Reader* (Durham: Duke University Press, 2001), 505–18.

2. Andy Crouch, *The Tech-Wise Family: Everyday Steps for Putting Technology in Its Proper Place* (Grand Rapids: Baker Books, 2017).

3. Presentation by Andy Crouch and Amy Crouch from their book *My Tech-Wise Life: Growing Up and Making Choices in a World of Devices* (Grand Rapids: Baker Books, 2020) for the North Carolina Study Center, December 10, 2020.

4. See Andy Crouch, "Eating the Supper of the Lamb in a Cool Whip Society: Albert Borgmann's Post-Technological Feast," *Books & Culture* 10, no. 1 (January/February 2004): https://www.booksandculture.com/articles/2004/janfeb/8.26.html. Another helpful introduction to Borgmann is his interview with David Wood. See David Wood, "Albert Borgmann on Taming Technology," *Christian Century*, August 23, 2003, 22–25.

5. Andy Crouch, presentation, Fleetwood Christian Reformed Church, Surrey, BC, October 5, 2016.

6. Albert Borgmann, *Technology and the Character of Contemporary Life: A Philosophical Inquiry* (Chicago: University of Chicago Press, 1984), 40–48.

7. Crouch, *Tech-Wise Family*, 41.

8. Borgmann, *Technology and the Character of Contemporary Life*, 37.

9. Borgmann, *Technology and the Character of Contemporary Life*, 37.

10. *Couples Retreat*, directed by Peter Billingsley, written by Jon Favreau, Vince Vaugh, and Dana Fox, released October 9, 2009.

11. Tim Perry tells this story about Dr. Geordie Rose's visit to Wycliffe College in Toronto in his forthcoming book *Funerals: For the Care of Souls* (Bellingham, WA: Lexham, forthcoming), 21.

12. See Jason Byassee, "If Death Is No Barrier," *Books & Culture* 13, no. 1 (January/February 2007), 16–21.

13. This point is often made by technology critic Jacques Ellul. See the summary and engagement in Jeffrey P. Greenman, Read Mercer Schuchardt, and Noah J. Toly, eds., *Understanding Jacques Ellul* (Eugene, OR: Cascade Books, 2012).

14. See Ruha Benjamin, *Race after Technology: Abolitionist Tools for the New Jim Code* (Medford, MA: Polity, 2019).

15. Robert Frost, "The Death of the Hired Man," Poetry Foundation, https://www.poetryfoundation.org/poems/44261/the-death-of-the-hired-man.

16. Crouch, *Tech-Wise Family*, 47–110, with a chapter devoted to each.

17. Crouch, *Tech-Wise Family*, 36.

18. Aaron White tells this story in his book *Recovering: From Brokenness and Addiction to Blessedness and Community* (Grand Rapids: Baker Academic, 2020), 27.

19. The stories related in the last several paragraphs come from an in-person interview with Cherie White on October 21, 2019.

20. Sven Birkerts, *The Gutenberg Elegies: The Fate of Reading in an Electronic Age* (New York: Farrar, Straus and Giroux, 1994), vii.

21. Birkerts, *Gutenberg Elegies*, 238–40.

22. Birkerts, *Gutenberg Elegies*, 234.

23. See "Sven Birkerts: Literary Culture in the Electronic Age," *Faith & Leadership* (December 14, 2009): https://faithandleadership.com/sven-birkerts-literary-culture-elec tronic-age.

24. "Official University of Michigan Masturbation Policy," posted by u/f0xmulder, January 25, 2008, https://www.reddit.com/r/funny/comments/ad14n/official_university_of _michigan_masturbation; "University of Michigan Poster," *Huff Post*, December 6, 2017, https://www.huffpost.com/entry/masturbation-university-m_n_382536.

25. Elizabeth Gilbert, *The Last American Man* (New York: Penguin, 2003).

26. Gilbert, *Last American Man*, 70–72.

27. The stories recounted here come from a Zoom interview with the Perrys, conducted July 17, 2020, and from a follow-up email conversation that took place August 9, 2020.

28. Baker Perry's work was recently featured by National Geographic both in their magazine and in a cable-TV special. See Freddie Wilkinson, "Inside the Everest Expedition That Built the World's Highest Weather Station," *National Geographic*, June 13, 2019, https:// www.nationalgeographic.com/adventure/2019/06/mount-everest-highest-weather-station.

29. As of 2018, the birth rate in North America was 1.7 births per woman, and the European Union was at 1.5. "Fertility Rate, Total (Births per Woman)," The World Bank, 2018, https://data.worldbank.org/indicator/SP.DYN.TFRT.IN.

Chapter 5 Undistracted Friendship

1. Shainnah Ali, "What You Need to Know about the Loneliness Epidemic," *Psychology Today*, July 12, 2018, https://www.psychologytoday.com/ca/blog/modern-mental ity/201807/what-you-need-know-about-the-loneliness-epidemic.

2. Quoted in Emma Seppälä, "Empathy Is on the Decline in This Country," *Washington Post*, June 11, 2019, https://www.washingtonpost.com/lifestyle/2019/06/11/empathy-is -decline-this-country-new-book-describes-what-we-can-do-bring-it-back.

3. Elisa Gabbert, "Is Compassion Fatigue Inevitable in an Age of 24-Hour News?," *The Guardian*, August 2, 2018, https://www.theguardian.com/news/2018/aug/02/is-compassion -fatigue-inevitable-in-an-age-of-24-hour-news.

4. Cal Newport, "Steve Jobs Never Wanted Us to Use Our iPhones Like This," *New York Times*, January 25, 2019, https://www.nytimes.com/2019/01/25/opinion/sunday/steve -jobs-never-wanted-us-to-use-our-iphones-like-this.html.

5. Isaac Stanley-Becker, "Horns Are Growing on Young People's Skulls. Phone Use Is to Blame, Research Suggests," *Washington Post*, June 25, 2019, https://www.washington post.com/nation/2019/06/20/horns-are-growing-young-peoples-skulls-phone-use-is-blame -research-suggests.

6. See Jacob Roshgadol, "Quarantine Quality Time: 4 in 5 Parents Say Coronavirus Lockdown Has Brought Family Closer Together," Study Finds, April 21, 2020, https:// www.studyfinds.org/quarantine-quality-time-4-in-5-parents-say-coronavirus-lockdown -has-brought-family-closer-together; Josh Anderer, "The Bright Side: Coronavirus Is Bringing Communities, Couples Closer Together," Study Finds, March 24, 2020, https://

www.studyfinds.org/the-bright-side-coronavirus-is-bringing-communities-couples-closer
-together; Helen Fisher, "How Coronavirus Is Changing the Dating Game for the Better,"
New York Times, May 7, 2020, https://www.nytimes.com/2020/05/07/well/mind/dating
-coronavirus-love-relationships.html.

7. Sebastian Maniscalco, *What's Wrong with People?*, directed by Manny Rodriguez,
released January 5, 2012, on Netflix, 1:15:31, here 16:00.

8. Glennon Doyle, *Untamed* (New York: Random House, 2020), 260.

9. Adam Gazzaley and Larry D. Rosen, *The Distracted Mind: Ancient Brains in a
High-Tech World* (Cambridge, MA: MIT Press, 2016), 120.

10. William Deresiewicz, "Faux Friendship," *Chronicle of Higher Education*, December
6, 2009, https://www.chronicle.com/article/Faux-Friendship/49308.

11. Jack Johnson, "Flake," track 5 on *Brushfire Fairytales*, Enjoy Records, 2001.

12. Aristotle's discussion of friendship can be found in book 8 of his *Nicomachean
Ethics*, trans. W. D. Ross, The Internet Classics Archive, http://classics.mit.edu/Aristotle
/nicomachaen.html.

13. Rana el Kaliouby, *Girl Decoded: A Scientist's Quest to Reclaim Our Humanity by
Bringing Emotional Intelligence to Technology* (New York: Currency, 2020), 270.

14. Deresiewicz, "Faux Friendship."

15. Email correspondence, June 24, 2020.

16. Sarah Coakley, *God, Sexuality, and the Self: An Essay 'On the Trinity'* (Cambridge:
Cambridge University Press, 2013), 316.

17. Naomi Wolf, "The Porn Myth," *New York Magazine*, October 9, 2003, https://
nymag.com/nymetro/news/trends/n_9437.

18. Yes, I will tell you how to do this: hover over your image and click on the ellipsis
that appears. Select "hide self view." Never look back.

Chapter 6 The Internet Is (Kind of) a Place

1. William Carey, *An Enquiry into the Obligations of Christians* (Leicester: Ann Ireland,
1792), 8, https://www.wmcarey.edu/carey/enquiry/anenquiry.pdf.

2. In 2018 the United Church of Canada approved a major governance and structural
shift, saving an estimated eleven million dollars over a three-year period, which could
be redistributed for the sake of keeping congregational doors open. "United in God's
Work," The United Church of Canada, March 2015, http://252171b255e88fd7c65a-dec
189f157202212a76b23fc4d185c40.r92.cf2.rackcdn.com/crtg_report.pdf, 30–33.

3. For more information on these movements, visit their websites: Fresh Expressions,
https://freshexpressions.org.uk; EDGE, https://edge-ucc.ca.

4. Sallie McFague, *Blessed Are the Consumers: Climate Change and the Practice of
Restraint* (Minneapolis: Fortress, 2013), 27.

5. That's ESPN for those of you south of the border . . .

6. "Draw the Circle Wide" is a song by The Common Cup Company, sung throughout
the mainline church as an expression of our inclusive ethos (bonus if there are tambourines
involved). "Come to the Altar" is an Elevation Worship (Furtick's church) original, expressing salvation from one's sins through Christ's blood (no tambourines, plenty of drums).

7. See Kristen French's article on DJ's church, "This Pastor Is Putting His Faith in a
Virtual Reality Church," *WIRED*, February 2, 2018, https://www.wired.com/story/virtual
-reality-church.

8. Philip Meadowsi, "Mission-Shaped Discipleship in Virtual World," *Wesleyan Theological Journal* 49, no. 2 (2014): 50.

9. Mary Oliver, "The Summer Day," in *New and Selected Poems: Volume One* (Boston: Beacon, 1992), 94.

10. Rich Villodas, Zoom interview, October 30, 2019.

11. Rich Villodas, Zoom interview, October 30, 2019.

12. Lesslie Newbigin, *Foolishness to the Greeks: The Gospel and Western Culture* (Grand Rapids: Eerdmans, 1986), 41.

13. Mark Rogers, "Broadcasting the Gospel," *Christianity Today*, March 2, 2010, https://www.christianitytoday.com/history/2010/march/broadcasting-gospel.html.

14. John MacArthur, "A Colossal Fraud," *Grace to You* (blog), December 7, 2009, https://www.gty.org/library/blog/B091207.

15. Max Roser, Hannah Ritchie, and Esteban Ortiz-Ospina, "Internet," Our World in Data, https://ourworldindata.org/internet.

16. Nilofer Merchant, "Feel Like You Don't Fit In? Here's How to Find Where You Truly Belong," Ideas.TED.com, August 30, 2017, https://ideas.ted.com/feel-like-you-dont-fit-in-heres-how-to-find-where-you-truly-belong.

17. See Ray Oldenburg, *The Great Good Place: Cafés, Coffee Shops, Bookstores, Bars, Hair Salons, and Other Hangouts at the Heart of Community* (New York: Marlowe & Co., 1989).

18. See Alvin Toffler, *Future Shock* (New York: Bantam, 1971).

19. David Nicholson, "The Pitfalls of a Brave New Cyberworld," *Washington Post National Weekly Edition*, October 9–15, 1995, p. 25.

20. J. Andrew Kirk, "Mission in the West: On the Calling of the Church in a Postmodern Age," in *A Scandalous Prophet: The Way of Mission after Newbigin*, ed. Thomas F. Foust, George R. Hunsberger, J. Andrew Kirk, and Werner Ustorf (Grand Rapids: Eerdmans, 2002), 124.

21. See Meadowsi, "Mission-Shaped Discipleship," 53.

22. Darrell L. Guder, *Missional Church: A Vision for the Sending of the Church in North America* (Grand Rapids: Eerdmans, 1998), 12.

Chapter 7 Virtual Virtue

1. This claim is common now, but I've been especially helped by Kevin Huddleston's DMin thesis "Sabbath as Mission: Engaging Families in the Mission of God through a Rhythm of Rest and Reflection" (DMin thesis, Lipscomb University, 2019), and Mark Scarlata's book *Sabbath Rest: The Beauty of God's Rhythm for a Digital Age* (London: SCM, 2019).

2. It's Rabbi Jonathan Sacks's way of putting it. See Jonathan Sacks, "Evolution or Revolution?," *Covenant & Conversation* (blog), May 13, 2019, http://rabbisacks.org/behar-5779.

3. Mark Glanville, *Adopting the Stranger as Kindred in Deuteronomy* (Atlanta: SBL Press, 2018), 83.

4. I take this claim from Will Willimon, who often points it out over against the enthusiastic general praise of Sabbath-keeping among pastors over the last generation or two.

5. Andy Crouch uses this terminology frequently, though he attributes this phrase to Tim Keller (Andy Crouch, "What's So Great about 'the Common Good'?," *Christianity Today*, October 12, 2012, https://www.christianitytoday.com/ct/2012/november/whats-so

-great-about-common-good.html). See also Andy Crouch, *Culture Making: Recovering Our Creative Calling* (Downers Grove, IL: IVP Books, 2008).

6. Andy Crouch, *The Tech-Wise Family: Everyday Steps for Putting Technology in Its Proper Place* (Grand Rapids: Baker Books, 2017), 81.

7. Crouch, *Tech-Wise Family*, 12.

8. Crouch, *Tech-Wise Family*, 13, 81. This point is made both by Amy Crouch in her foreword to the book and by Andy Crouch later in the book.

9. This is David Kinnaman's phrase from his book with Mark Matlock, *Faith for Exiles: 5 Ways for a New Generation to Follow Jesus in Digital Babylon* (Grand Rapids: Baker Books, 2019), 20.

10. Craig Gay, *Modern Technology and the Human Future: A Christian Appraisal* (Downers Grove, IL: IVP Academic, 2018), 20–22.

11. James K. A. Smith, "What God Knows: The Debate on 'Open Theism,'" *Christian Century*, July 12, 2005, https://www.christiancentury.org/article/2005-07/what-god-knows.

12. Brad Gregory, *The Unintended Reformation: How a Religious Revolution Secularized Society* (Cambridge, MA: Belknap, 2015), 57, quoted in Gay, *Modern Technology*, 118.

13. Gay makes this observation in his *Modern Technology*, 37.

14. Albert Borgmann, *Technology and the Character of Contemporary Life: A Philosophical Inquiry* (Chicago: University of Chicago Press, 1984), 196–209.

15. Borgmann, *Technology and the Character of Contemporary Life*, 103.

16. Borgmann, *Technology and the Character of Contemporary Life*, 177.

17. Borgmann, *Technology and the Character of Contemporary Life*, 219.

18. Borgmann, *Technology and the Character of Contemporary Life*, 151.

19. Gay, *Modern Technology*, 205–7.

20. Gay, *Modern Technology*, 206. See also Gay's "*No!*" on p. 183.

21. See Kinnaman and Matlock, *Faith for Exiles*.

22. Kinnaman and Matlock, *Faith for Exiles*, 71.

23. Kinnaman and Matlock, *Faith for Exiles*, 120.

24. Kinnaman and Matlock, *Faith for Exiles*, 140, 173–74.

25. Kinnaman and Matlock, *Faith for Exiles*, 193–96, pass on these Barna statistics: 64 percent of Gen Z Christians report that their church helps them have "courage to tell others about what [they] believe," and 56 percent say it helps with "wisdom for living with people who believe differently than [they do]."

26. For this Scripture reference, I'm grateful to John Dyer, *From the Garden to the City: The Redeeming and Corrupting Power of Technology* (Grand Rapids: Kregel, 2011), 30.

27. I owe this to Kathryn Recklis of the New Media Project. See "Give Me That Digital Religion," *The Immanent Frame*, March 3, 2015, https://tif.ssrc.org/2015/03/03/give-me -that-digital-religion.

28. Psalm 100, sung as "The Old Hundredth," acted as part of the Gathering during the inaugural service of the United Church of Canada. See William S. Kervin, ed., "The Inaugural Service (1925)," in *Ordered Liberty: Readings in the History of United Church Worship* (Toronto: United Church Publishing House, 2011), 15.

29. The quote from O'Neill comes from a Zoom interview conducted August 13, 2020.

30. John Cassian, *Conferences*, trans. Colm Luibheid (New York: Paulist Press, 1985), 2.26 (p. 79).

Chapter 8 Daring to Speak for God

1. These quotations are from an in-person interview conducted August 6, 2020, Sauder School of Business, Vancouver, BC.

2. In-person interview, Sauder School of Business, August 6, 2020.

3. Quoted in Richard Heitzenrater, *Wesley and the People Called Methodist*, 2nd ed. (Nashville: Abingdon, 2013), 109.

4. I owe this way of telling the story to a sermon by the Reverend Bonnie Scott, delivered April 27, 2011 at the Duke Divinity School chapel. You can watch it here: https://www.youtube.com/watch?v=UecUjIMoWtw.

5. This set of comments comes from an interview relating to Carnes's book *Image and Presence: Christological Reflection on Iconoclasm and Iconophilia* (Redwood City, CA: Stanford University Press, 2019): Amy Brown Hughes, "Natalie Carnes—Image and Presence," January 15, 2019, in *OnScript*, MP3 audio, 59:23, https://onscript.study/podcast/theology-natalie-carnes-image-and-presence.

6. Andy Crouch, Kurt Keilhacker, and David Blanchard, "Leading beyond the Blizzard: Why Every Organization Is Now a Startup," *The Praxis Journal*, March 20, 2020, https://journal.praxislabs.org/leading-beyond-the-blizzard-why-every-organization-is-now-a-startup-b7f32fb278ff.

7. These quotations are from a phone interview with Matt Miofsky conducted June 22, 2020.

Conclusion No Unmediated God

1. See, for example, Marshall McLuhan's book with Quentin Fiore, *The Medium Is the Massage: An Inventory of Effects* (Corte Madera, CA: Gingko, 2001).

2. This phrase is out there "in the ether" but is discussed by Fred Sanders at his blog: "The Kingdom in Person," *The Scriptorium Daily* (blog), July 28, 2015, http://scriptoriumdaily.com/the-kingdom-in-person. The comment comes from *Commentary of Origen on the Gospel of St. Matthew*, trans. Ronald Heine (Oxford: Oxford University Press, 2018).

3. This way of putting it purportedly comes from Mr. Wesley. I first heard it at Garrett Theological Seminary from Steve Long of Southern Methodist University.

4. Michael Wyschogrod, "Incarnation and God's Dwelling in Israel," in *Abraham's Promise: Judaism and Jewish-Christian Relations*, ed. R. Kendall Soulen (Grand Rapids: Eerdmans, 2004), 165–78.

5. Scott Chrostek, *The Misfit Mission: How to Change the World with Surprises, Interruption, and All the Wrong People* (Nashville: Abingdon, 2016), 141.

6. Willie James Jennings, *Acts: A Theological Commentary*, Belief (Louisville: Westminster John Knox, 2017), 102–14.

Index